Banjo Songs
Book with Online Audio Access

by
Geoff Hohwald

For access to the audio tracks for this course, go to this address on the internet:

cvls.com/extras/banjosongs/

ABOUT BANJO SONGS

Banjo Songs guides you straight to the heart of bluegrass banjo. Here are 96 arrangements that capture the true essence of banjo playing, those licks and breaks that make you turn your head and say, "Now *that* is what a banjo should sound like." This book will help you achieve *that* sound. You will improve the tone of your playing. You will improve your timing. You will improve the way you accent each note. By studying these arrangements and by playing along with the Audio Tracks, you will be the one turning heads.

Banjo Songs is not meant for the true beginner.* Perhaps you have been playing for six months and are ready to take your playing to the next level. Perhaps you have been playing for years, but feel that your style has become bland. Or perhaps you are a teacher in search of new instructional material. If you fall in any of these three groups, then this book is for you.

Banjo Songs is designed to help you sound like a professional, but has been written with the knowledge that you are not, in fact, a professional. There are several arrangements for most of the songs, each constructed with varying degrees of complexity, and each recorded at two different speeds. The idea is not simply to memorize the songs. Through careful study you will see how many of these breaks and licks can be used in everything you play. By learning one song you will, in essence, be learning many songs.

HOW TO USE BANJO SONGS

Beginner/Intermediate: It is not necessary to practice the material in the order presented. That said, it is probably a good idea to start with the easiest arrangement, learn it completely, and then move on to the more complicated pieces.
Breakdown the breakdowns. That is, if you are having difficulty with a particular measure, spend a few days practicing just that portion of the arrangement.

Intermediate/Advanced: Practice the arrangements in any order you like. You may want to incorporate parts of these arrangements with other arrangements you already know. Also, try taking a lick or break from one song and using it within the context of another song.

The Audio Tracks: All of the music in **Banjo Songs** is played on the Audio Tracks. Each song is played at two speeds: slow for practicing, and up-tempo for performing. Each song is on an individual track to make it easy to locate.

* For the true beginner, we recommend the Banjo Primer Deluxe Edition Book with DVD and 2 Jam CDs.

ABOUT THE AUTHOR

Geoff Hohwald has played and taught the banjo for more than forty years. He originally studied with the likes of John Hickman and Robbie Robinson and later came under the influence of other legendary performers such as Earl Scruggs, Bill Keith, J.D. Crowe and Sonny Osborne. Geoff wrote his first instructional book in 1979, and since then he and Bert Casey have sold over three million books, videos, and DVDs worldwide.

Geoff spent thirty years and traveled thousands of miles in a quest for the licks that capture the true essence of bluegrass banjo. For the first time he has compiled the results of a lifetime of listening, searching, analyzing, and refining in a single edition.

He would like to thank Billy McKinley, Sandy Rothman, Herb Trotman, Ted Billeadeaux, Tom Dew, Mike Mason, Judge Parker, Kerry Warbington, Joe Zalik, and Harry Sparks.

Thanks also to:

Toby Ruckert at Toby Tone Studios for the recording.
Bert Casey for the final revisions and mastering.
Tim Wimer for the notation.
Leonard Wortzel for the introduction.
Debra Vercammen for the art work.
Peter Vogl for encouraging me to play with a metronome.

DEDICATION

This book is dedicated to my children, Andy and Sarah.

ONLINE AUDIO ACCESS

For access to the online audio tracks for this course, go to this address on the internet:

cvls.com/extras/banjosongs/

TABLE OF CONTENTS

SECTION 1
GETTING STARTED

For access to the audio tracks for this course, go to this address on the web:

cvls.com/extras/banjosongs/

TUNING THE BANJO

Before playing the banjo, it must be tuned to standard pitch. If you have a piano at home, it can be used as a tuning source. The following picture shows which note on the piano to tune each open string of the banjo to.

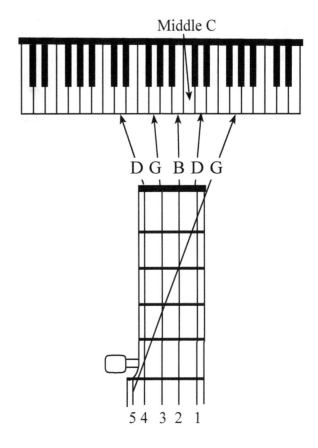

Note - If your piano hasn't been tuned recently, the banjo may not agree perfectly with a pitch pipe or tuning fork. Some older pianos are tuned a half step below standard.

PITCH PIPES

Pitch pipes are an easy and portable way of tuning a banjo. They may be obtained at a local music store with complete instructions.

AUDIO TRACKS

It is recommended that you tune your banjo to the Audio Tracks that accompanies this book so that you will be in tune when you play along with the songs and exercises.

ELECTRONIC TUNER

If you can afford one, an electronic tuner is the fastest and most accurate way to tune a banjo. I highly recommend getting one. They are available for $30 - $50.

RELATIVE TUNING

Relative tuning is used to tune the banjo to itself when you don't have an electronic tuner.

1. Tune the 4th string to a D using a pitch pipe or other source.

2. Note the 4th string at the 5th fret. Tune the 3rd string until it sounds like the 4th string at the 5th fret.

3. Note the 3rd string at the 4th fret. Tune the 2nd string until it sounds like the 3rd string at the 4th fret.

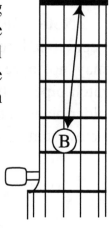

4. Note the 2nd string at the 3rd fret. Tune the 1st string until it sounds like the 2nd string at the 3rd fret.

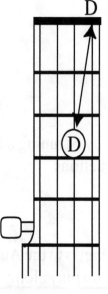

5. Note the 1st string at the 5th fret. Tune the 5th string until it sounds like the 1st string at the 5th fret.

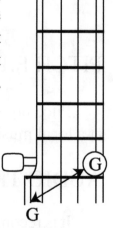

TABLATURE

Tablature is a system for writing music which shows the proper string and fret to play as well as the correct fingers to use.

In banjo tablature, each space represents a string on the banjo:

1st string
2nd string
3rd string
4th string
5th string

If the string is to be noted, the fret number is written in the appropriate space, otherwise an (0) is written. Here are several examples:

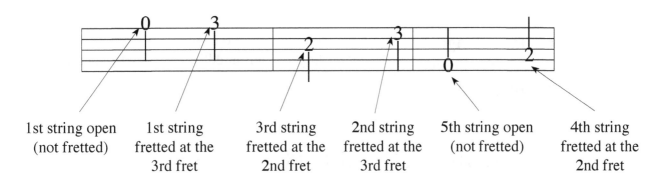

| 1st string open (not fretted) | 1st string fretted at the 3rd fret | 3rd string fretted at the 2nd fret | 2nd string fretted at the 3rd fret | 5th string open (not fretted) | 4th string fretted at the 2nd fret |

RIGHT HAND FINGERING

The correct finger of the right hand is written below the lines as shown below:

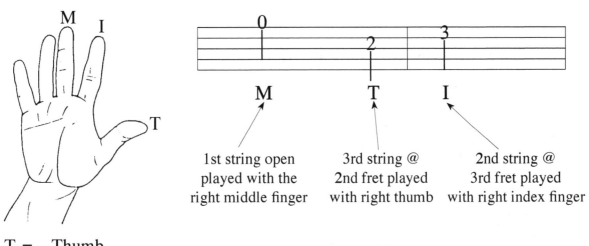

1st string open played with the right middle finger

3rd string @ 2nd fret played with right thumb

2nd string @ 3rd fret played with right index finger

T = Thumb
I = Index Finger
M = Middle Finger

LEFT HAND FINGERING

Fingering is also written above the tablature. These are the recommended left hand fingerings for certain passages as shown below:

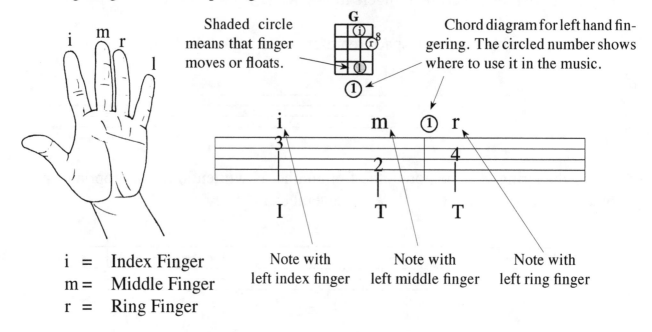

Shaded circle means that finger moves or floats.

Chord diagram for left hand fingering. The circled number shows where to use it in the music.

Note with left index finger

Note with left middle finger

Note with left ring finger

i = Index Finger
m = Middle Finger
r = Ring Finger

HAMMER-ON, SLIDE, PULL-OFF, CHOKE

The notation for hammer on, pull off, slide, and choke is shown as follows:

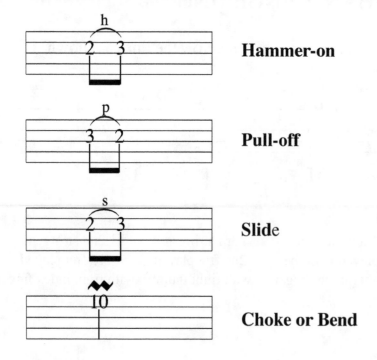

Hammer-on

Pull-off

Slide

Choke or Bend

TIMING

Musical notes are divided into equal time segments. In this example, there are 4 beats per measure and each is divided in half. Each line represents 1/2 beat (eighth note).

Most notes in this book are held for either 1 or 1/2 beat.

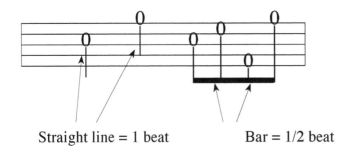

Straight line = 1 beat   Bar = 1/2 beat

Just count out the appropriate value for each note (1/2 beat or 1 beat).

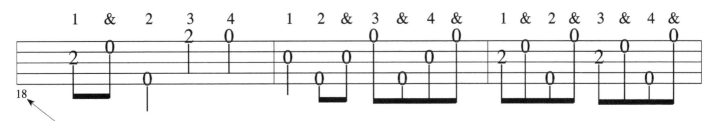

The first measure of each line of tab is numbered for easy reference.

Play along with the Audio Tracks on all the music examples to make sure you play with the proper timing.

Chord diagrams are used throughout the book to show the finger positions of the left hand. A shaded circle means that finger moves or floats. The circled number shows the position in the music to use the chord.

The different breaks or solos for banjo often have lead in notes or kick off notes that start before beat 1 of the 1st measure. The arrow shows where to start the kick off for the break.

SECTION 2
THE SONGS

For access to the audio tracks for this course, go to this address on the web:

cvls.com/extras/banjosongs/

CRIPPLE CREEK

Arr. by Geoff Hohwald

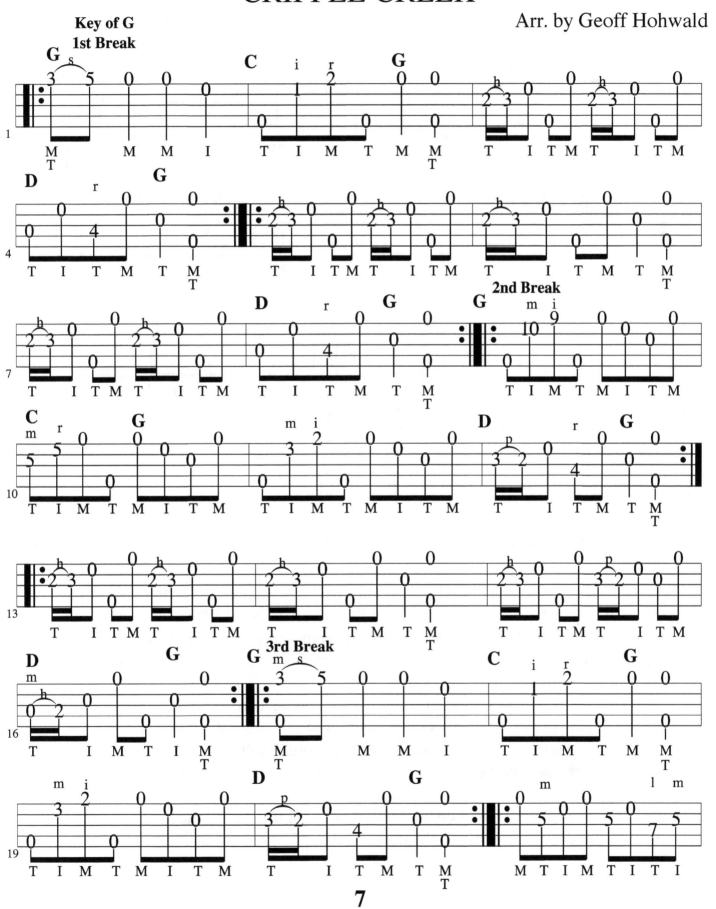

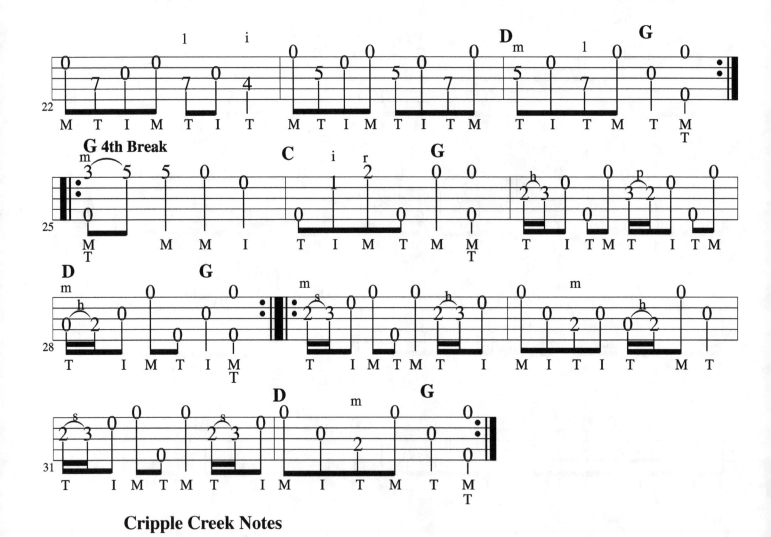

Cripple Creek Notes

Cripple Creek is included because most banjoists are familiar with the tune, particularly if they have worked through the *Banjo Primer* book. We've included several variations to make it more interesting. When learning these variations remember that we can mix and match. For example, measures 5 through 8 can be substituted for measures 13 through 16 or vice versa.

There will be notes on each song to give you background and insight into the arrangements in this book. This is in addition to the chord diagrams and left hand fingerings which will help you in playing the more difficult measures. Don't worry if things aren't perfect. Some of these techniques will take years to perfect, but don't give up.

Notice there are 4 tracks on the Audio Tracks for this song. The fast version (120 bpm) is divided into 2 parts and the slow version (35 bpm) is also divided into 2 parts.

OLD JOE CLARK

Arr. by Geoff Hohwald

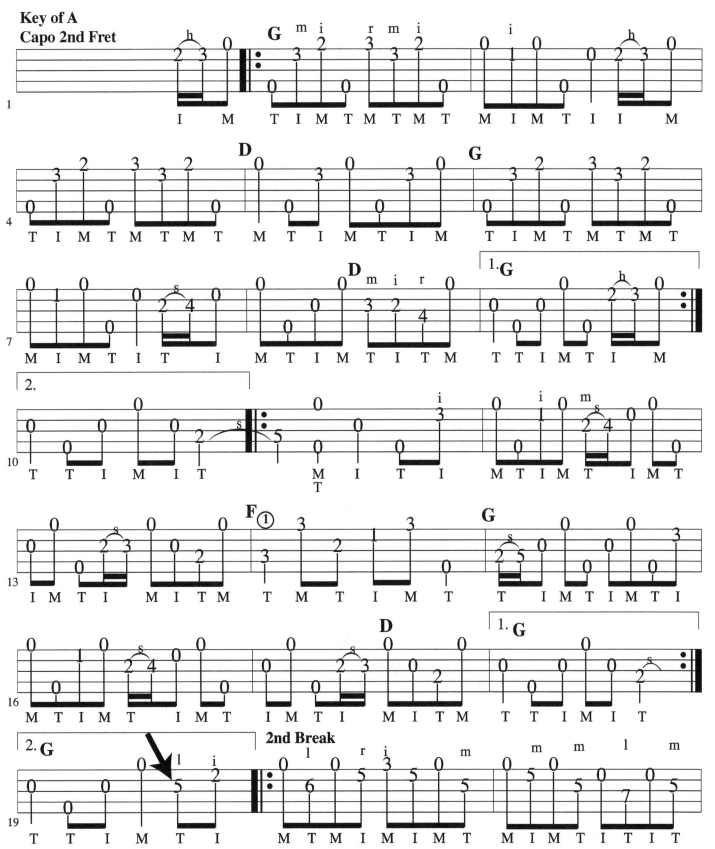

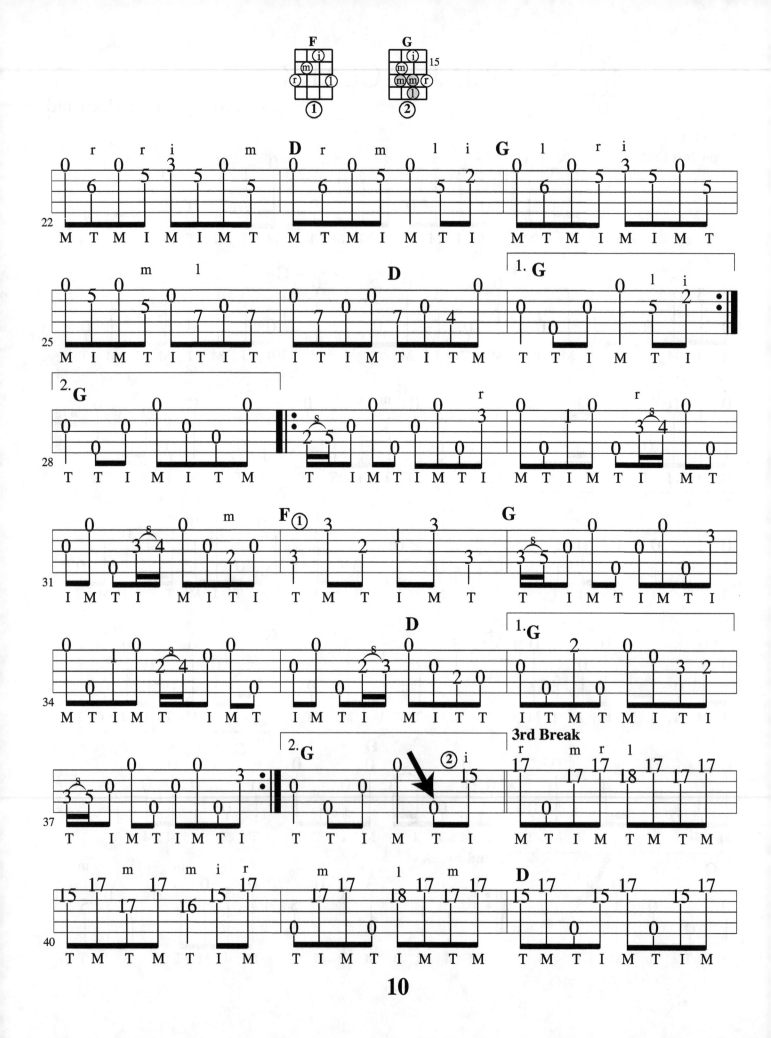

10

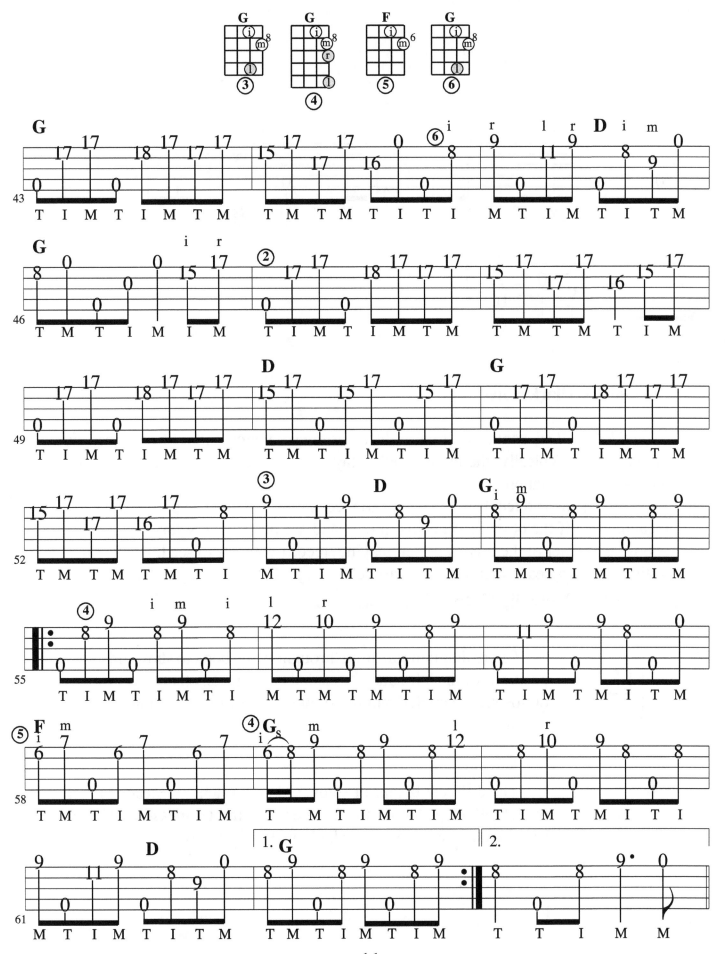

11

Ending

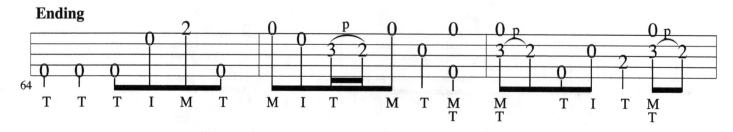

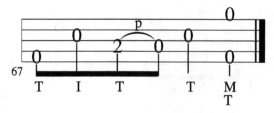

Old Joe Clark Notes

Old Joe Clark contains 3 totally different breaks which should be focused on individually. Typically, the banjo would play 2 breaks with a band, meaning you have an extra variation.

You will also notice there is a wide variance in how fast you can play each break, meaning that if the other instruments in the band are playing very fast, you should choose the easier of the breaks. When playing, record yourself to see how clear and in time you play each measure of a particular song. This will let you know where you need to focus your practice time.

Chord diagrams are used throughout the book to show the finger positions of the left hand. A shaded circle means that finger moves or floats. The circled number shows the position in the music to use the chord.

The different breaks or solos for banjo often have lead in notes or kick off notes that start before beat 1 of the 1st measure. The arrow shows where to start the kick off for the break.

NINE POUND HAMMER

Arr. by Geoff Hohwald

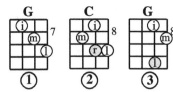

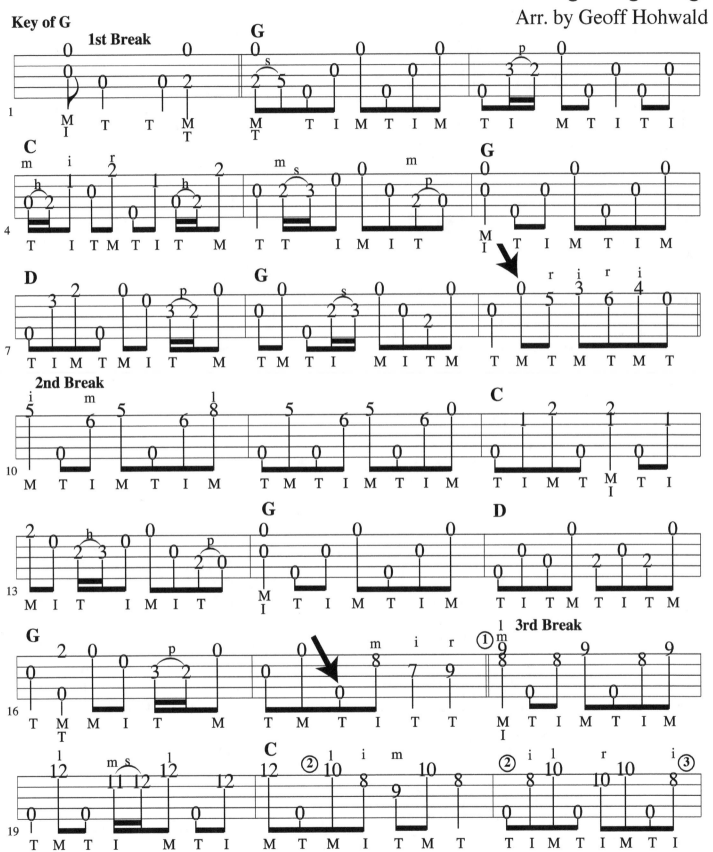

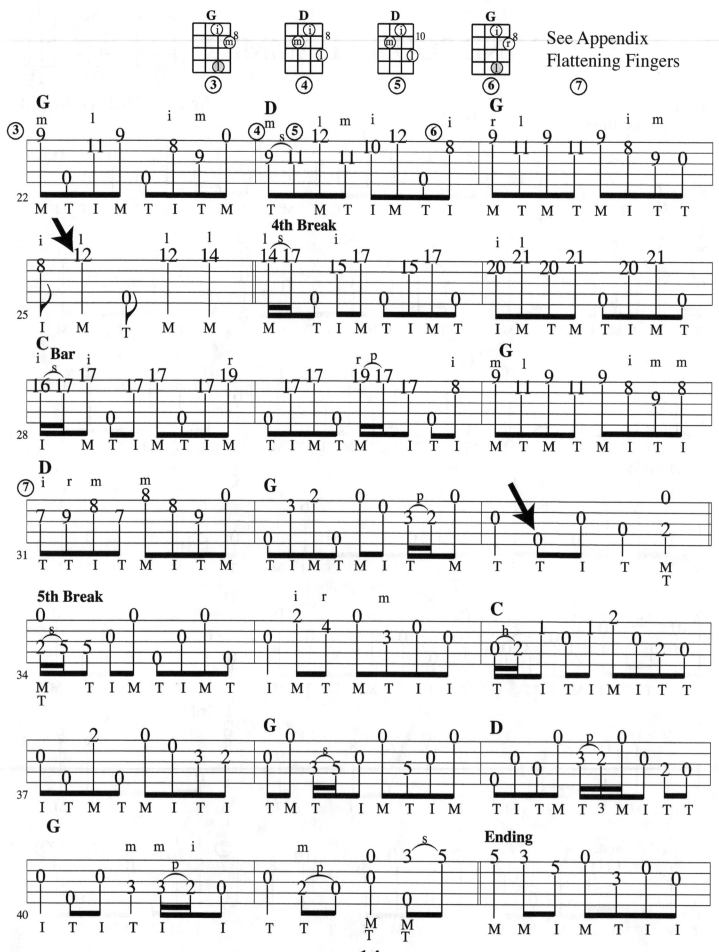

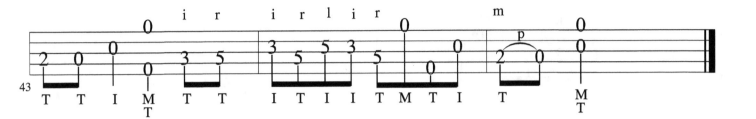

Nine Pound Hammer Notes

Measure 5 - Listen to the pull off, which is the last 2 notes of measure 5.

Measures 9,10,11 - The chromatic lead in measures 9,10,11 needs to be played clearly to be effective.

Measure 25 - We are using the left hand index finger to note the 2nd string @ 8th fret and the little finger to note the 1st string @ 12th fret. Practice measure 25 over and over focusing on the first two notes.

Measure 29 - Watch for a clear pull off.

Measure 30 - Isolate this measure and practice it separately, particularly the last 2 notes which involve using the left hand middle finger twice in a row. You will notice that *Nine Pound Hammer* is played at a variety of speeds, depending on who you are playing with. As the speed increases, focus more on the easier licks and breaks so that you can play with clarity.

For access to the audio tracks for this course, go to this address on the web:

cvls.com/extras/banjosongs/

WILL THE CIRCLE BE UNBROKEN

Key of G
1st Break

Arr. by Hohwald & Trotman

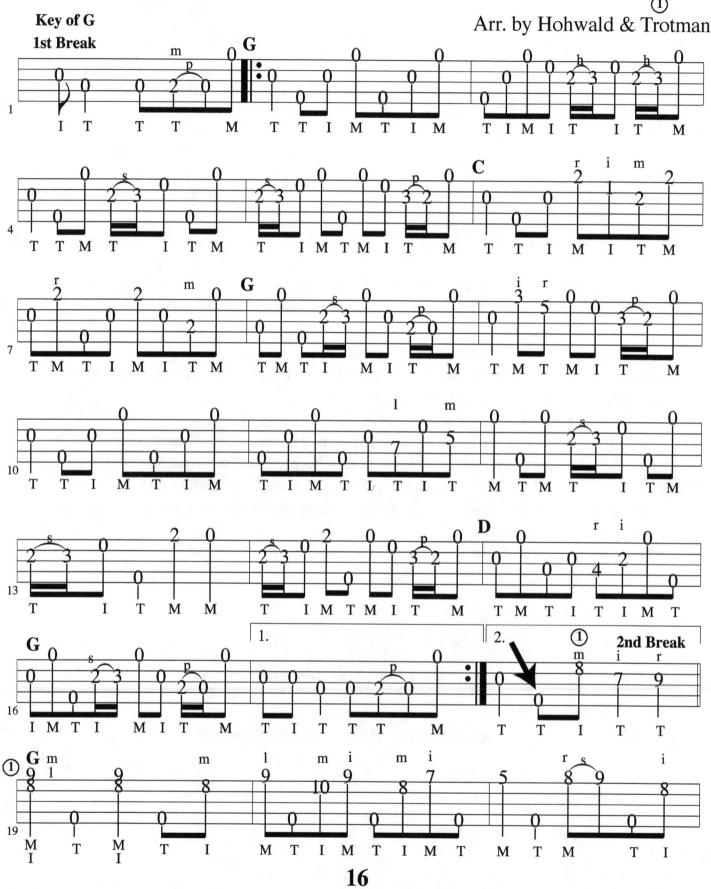

16

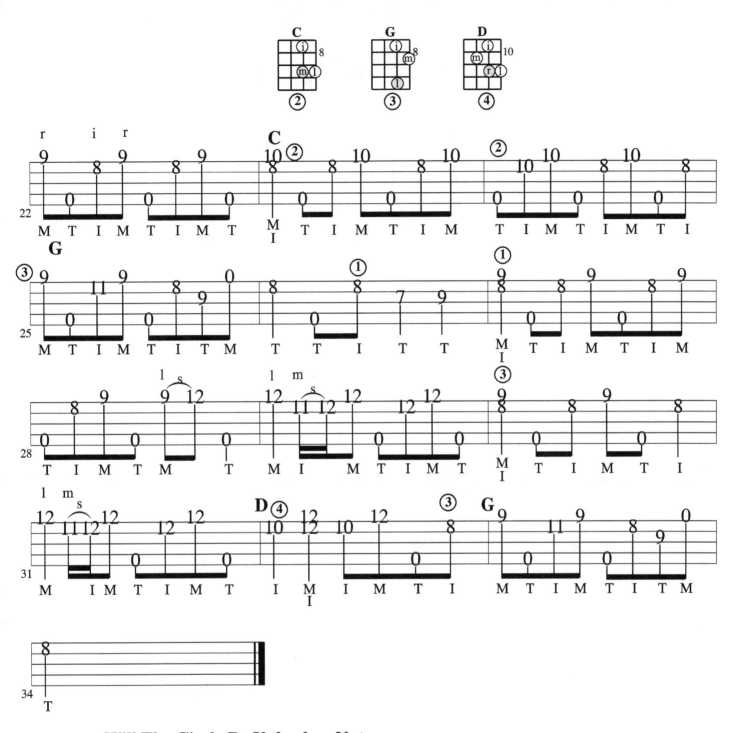

Will The Circle Be Unbroken Notes

Before trying to play up the neck breaks, you should make sure you understand the left hand fingerings. It should be efficient and flow smoothly. Studying the second break will give you a lot of insight into left hand movement. Pay close attention to the fingerings and chord diagrams. Pay special attention to the left little finger in measures 28, 29, and 31. Notice in measure 26 how the left index and middle finger switch to note the 2nd string 8th fret, which is the first and third note of the measure.

AMAZING GRACE

Arr. by Geoff Hohwald

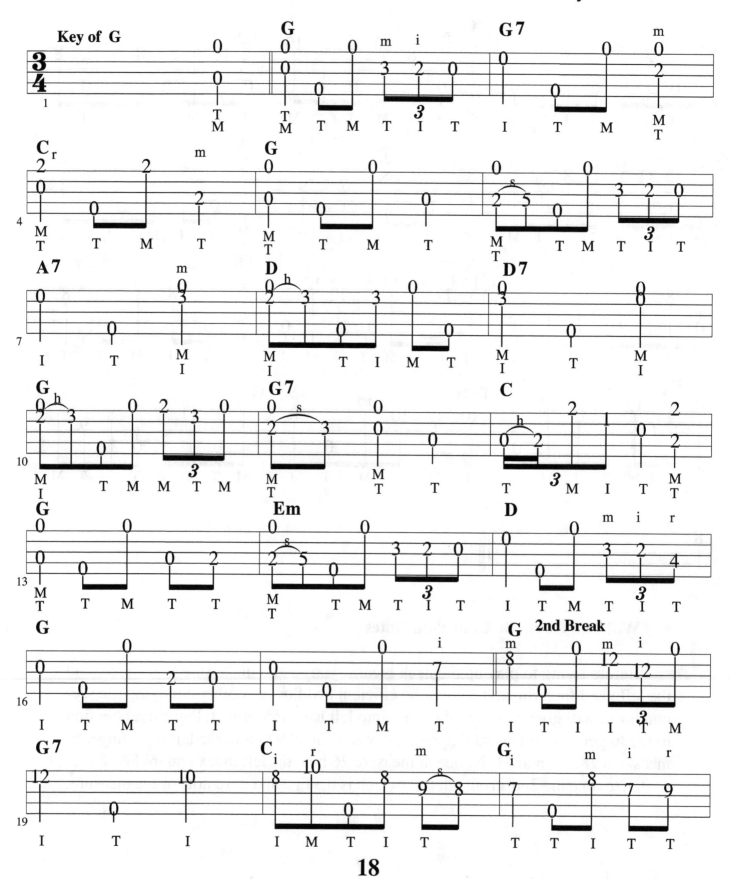

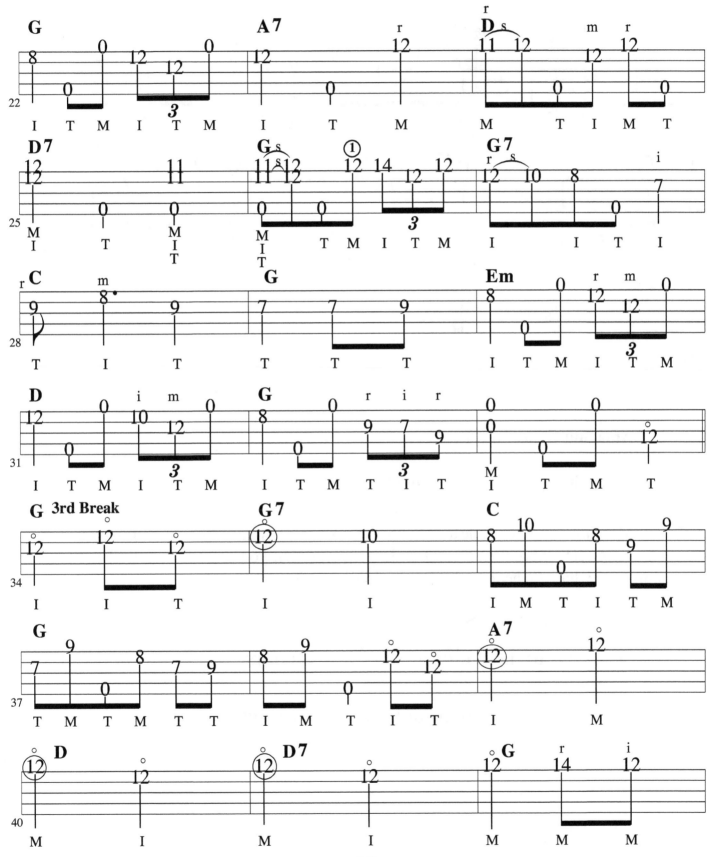

19

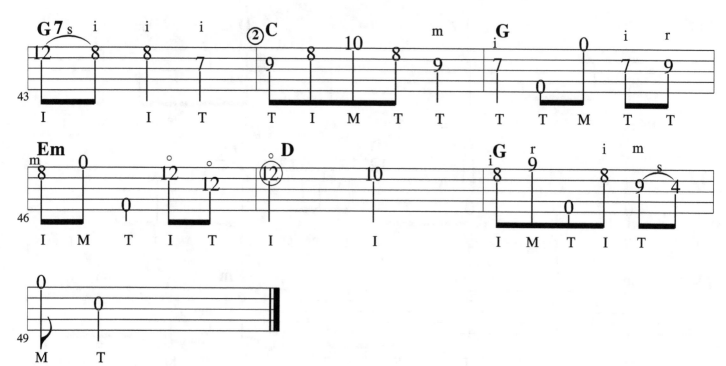

Amazing Grace Notes

Watch the right and left hand fingerings.

Measure 34 - To execute a chime or harmonic (ₒ), lightly touch the string you're playing directly above the fret wire. Experiment until you get a clear bell like tone similar to what you hear on the companion Audio Tracks.

For access to the audio tracks for this course, go to this address on the web:

cvls.com/extras/banjosongs/

PRETTY POLLY

Arr. by Geoff Hohwald

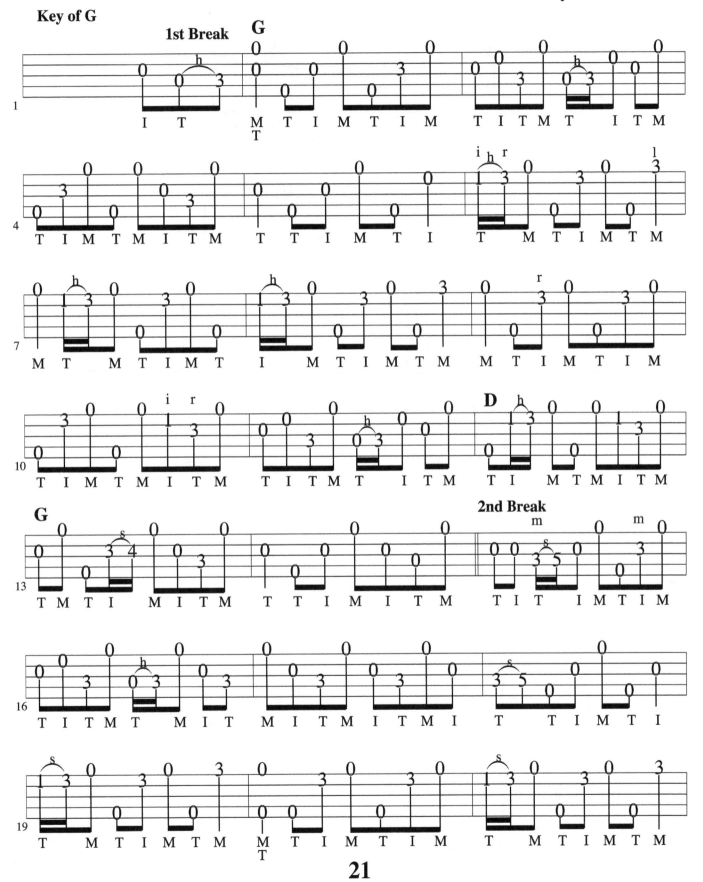

21

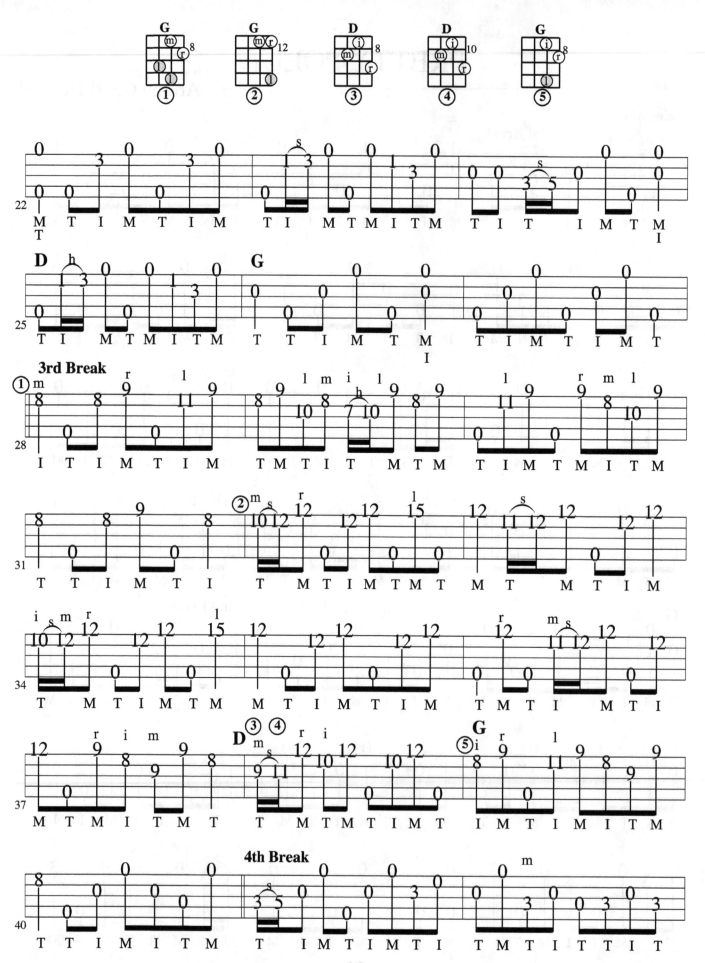

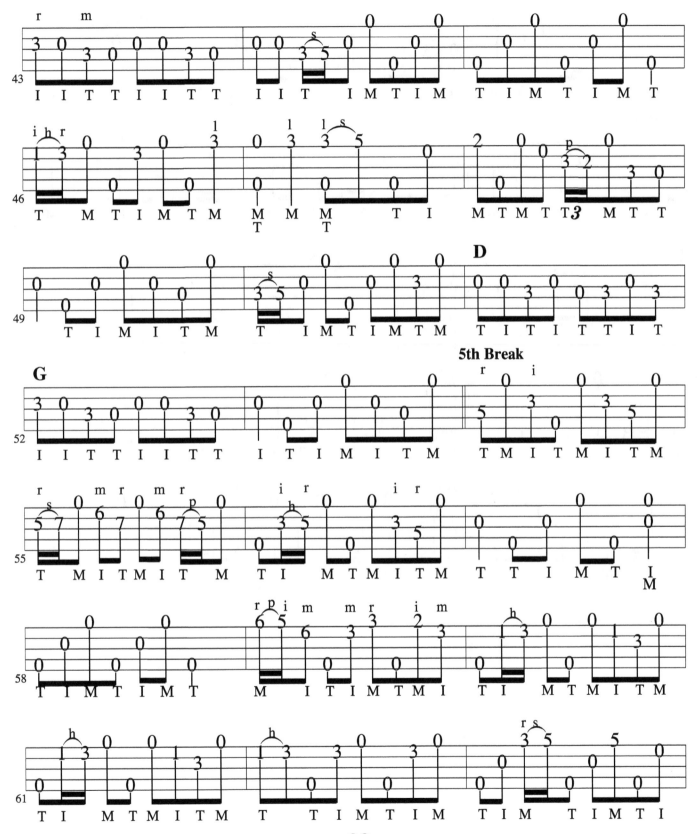

23

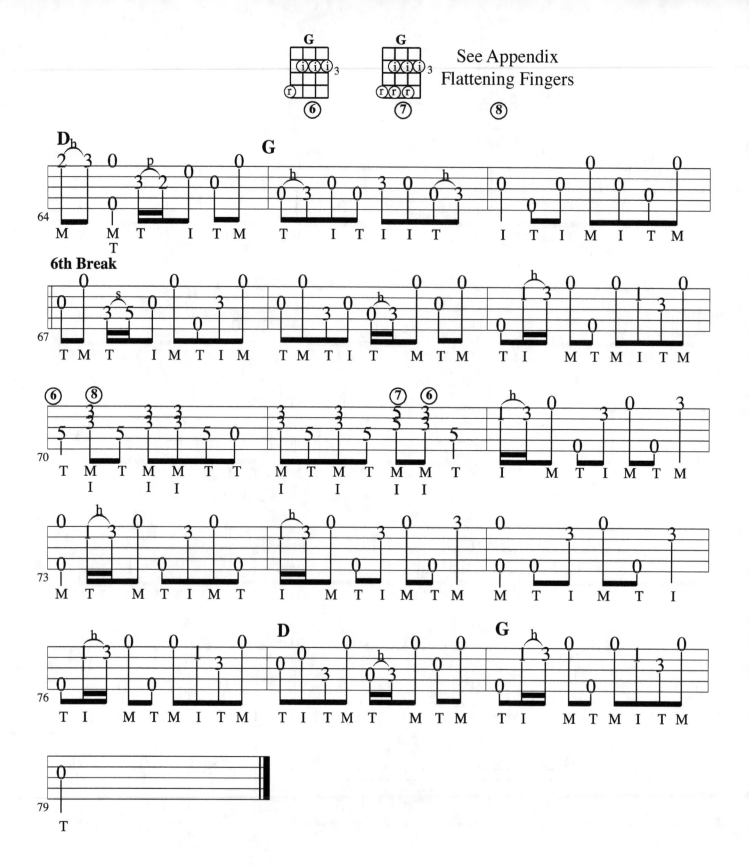

See Appendix
Flattening Fingers

6th Break

Turn to the next page for notes on *Pretty Polly*.

24

Pretty Polly Notes

Listen to measures 2 and 4 on the Audio Tracks. You will notice that by slightly bending upward on the 3rd string at the 3rd fret, you will get a better sound.

In measures 16 and 17, when noting the 4th string 3rd fret, the left middle finger lifts up after noting each note so that the note does not sustain or ring.

In measure 24, the 3rd string open is played twice in a row to give a percussive feel. To hear the difference, play the measure this time using the 2nd string open as the second note of the measure instead of the 3rd string open.

In measure 29, the little finger is used to hammer on the 3rd string 10th fret, which is very difficult, if not impossible for most people. In order to practice this, I recommend capoing the banjo to A at the 2nd fret or B at the 4th fret. This results in 2 things:

1. The frets are closer together, resulting in an easier reach.

2. The capo pulls the strings closer to the fret board, making them easier to note.

As your fingers stretch, you can then play without a capo. I recommend using a capo anytime the left hand is having difficulty stretching for the notes.

As in any up the neck break, make sure you are using the correct left hand fingering. If you still cannot play the hammer on, omit it and play the 3rd string 7th fret instead of the hammer on.

In measures 42 & 43 and 51 & 53 we use both the index finger and thumb of the right hand twice in a row.

Practice the following separately:

1. Measure 54
2. Measure 55
3. Measure 54 and 55
4. Measure 59(Include the first note of measure 60)
5. Measure 63
6. Measure 64
7. Measures 63 and 64 combined
8. Measure 65

Measures 70 and 71 are explained in the Appendix.

SWING LOW, SWEET CHARIOT

Arr. by Geoff Hohwald

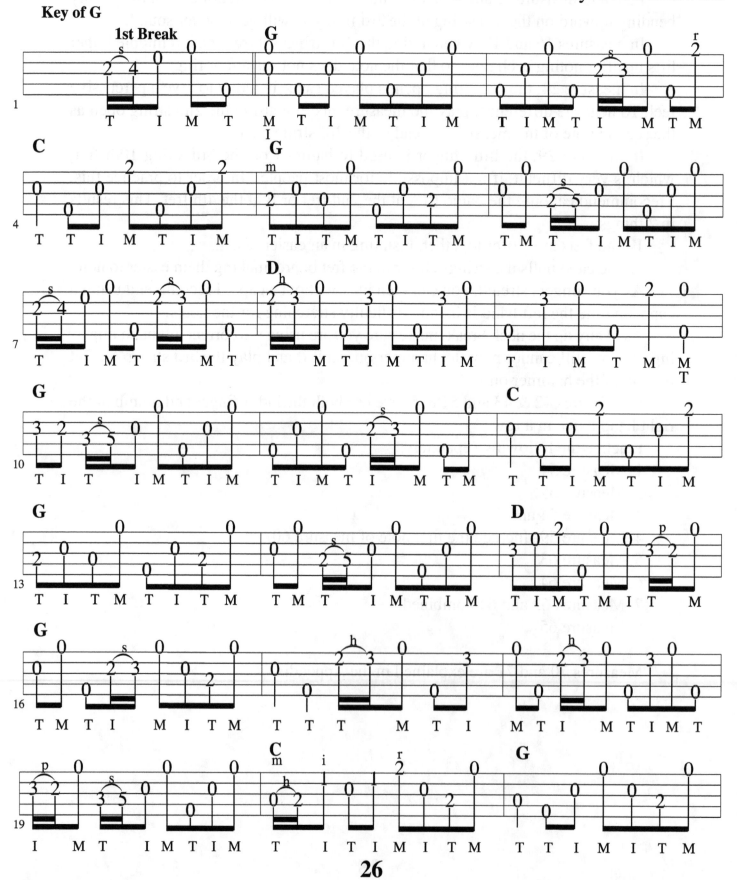

26

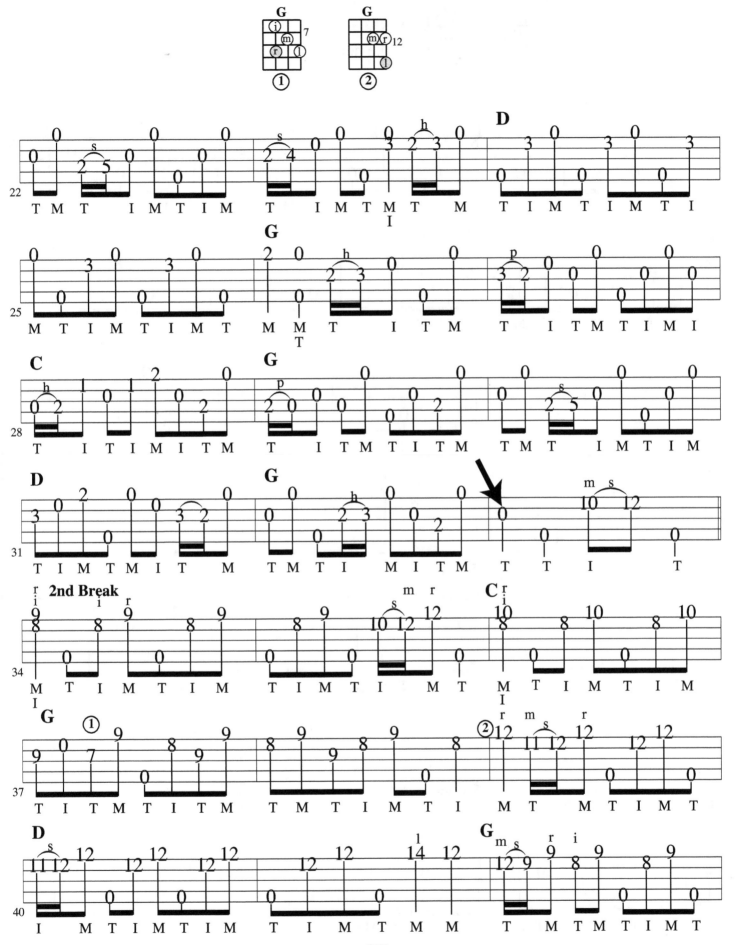

27

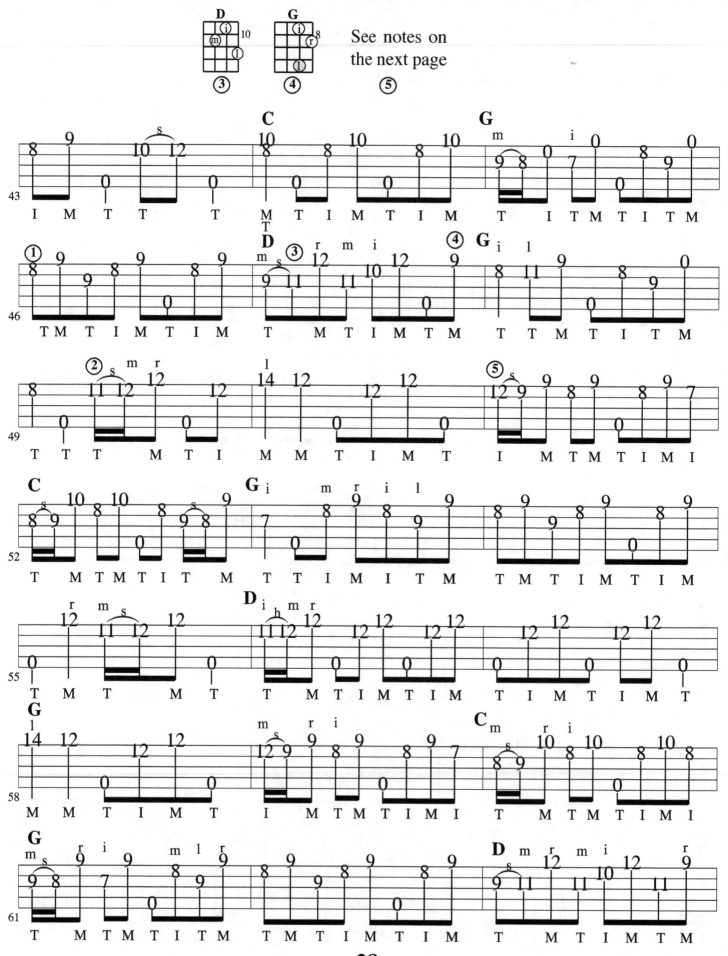

See notes on
the next page

28

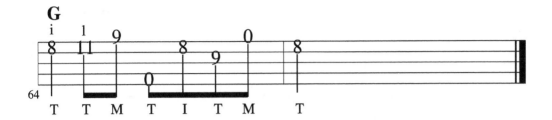

Swing Low, Sweet Chariot Notes

There is a lot of left hand movement in measures 51 & 52 as shown below:

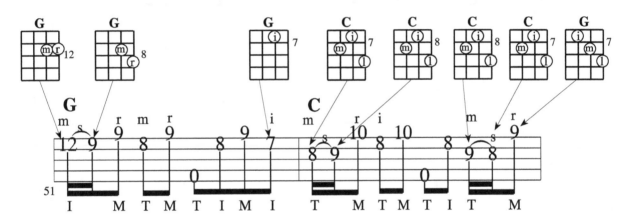

Practice these two measures over and over until you can play smoothly with the correct fingerings.

Break 1 - This is a pretty straight forward break. I particularly like the rhythm of measures 17 and 18 and measures 23 through 27.

Break 2 will function as another study in moving the left hand. To aid in your study, consult the fingerings and diagrams and the Appendix on page 106. Studying this break will give you information and experience, which will help with other songs. Practice slowly to promote clarity. Both breaks to *Swing Low Sweet Chariot* sound great if played clearly.

Measure 61 - Look at the end of measure 52 and 53 to see similarities between these and Measure 61.

Measure 63 - This is similar to measure 47. If you need further insight, this may be an excellent time to consult a teacher.

SOLDIER'S JOY

Arr. by Geoff Hohwald

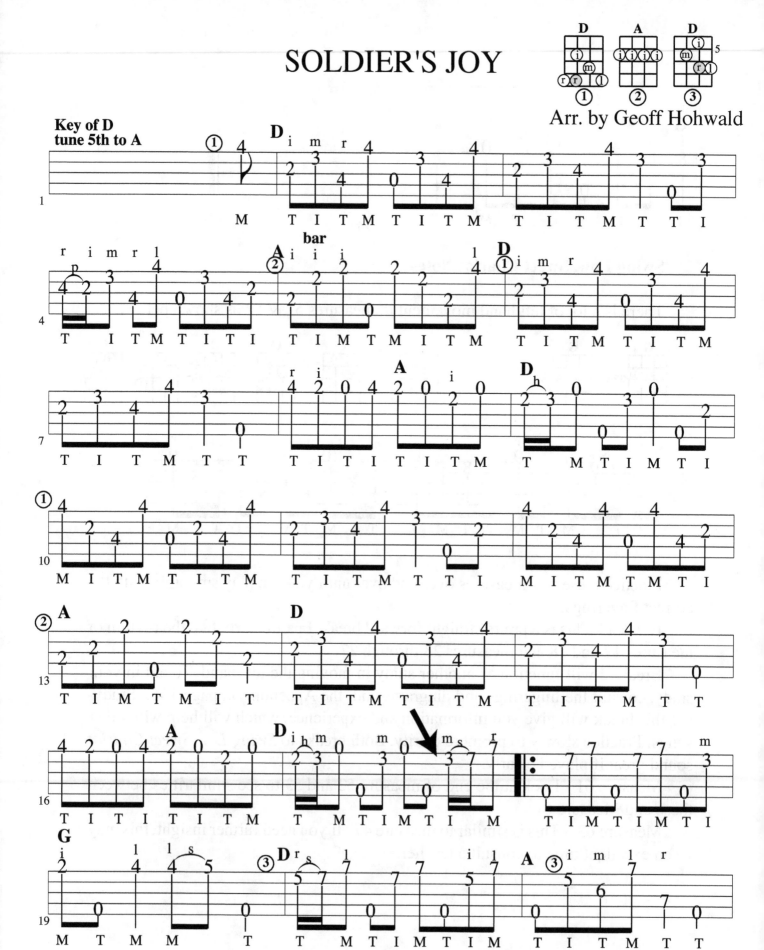

30

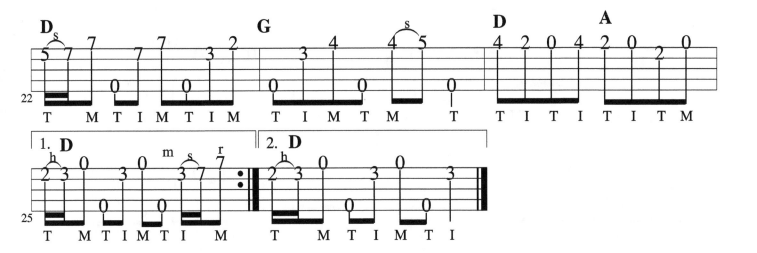

Soldier's Joy Notes

This version of *Soldier's Joy* is played out of the D position and is fairly straight forward. Watch the left hand fingerings. For most of the 1st Break, a D shape is held (Chord 1).

Measure 8 - We play several notes on the same string, alternating between the right thumb and index fingers.

The left hand fingerings in measures 19 & 20 set up Chord 3 in measure 21.

Fisher's Hornpipe Notes

The main goal of this song is clarity. Play the notes accurately and let the open strings sustain or ring. As you move the left hand from position to position, it is very easy to hit adjacent strings, either making strange sounds or stopping them from ringing.

Measure 13 is particularly difficult.

Measure 14 and 15 - Notice the fingering going from the last note of measure 14 to all of measure 15. Isolate the hard parts of this song and put most of your practice there.

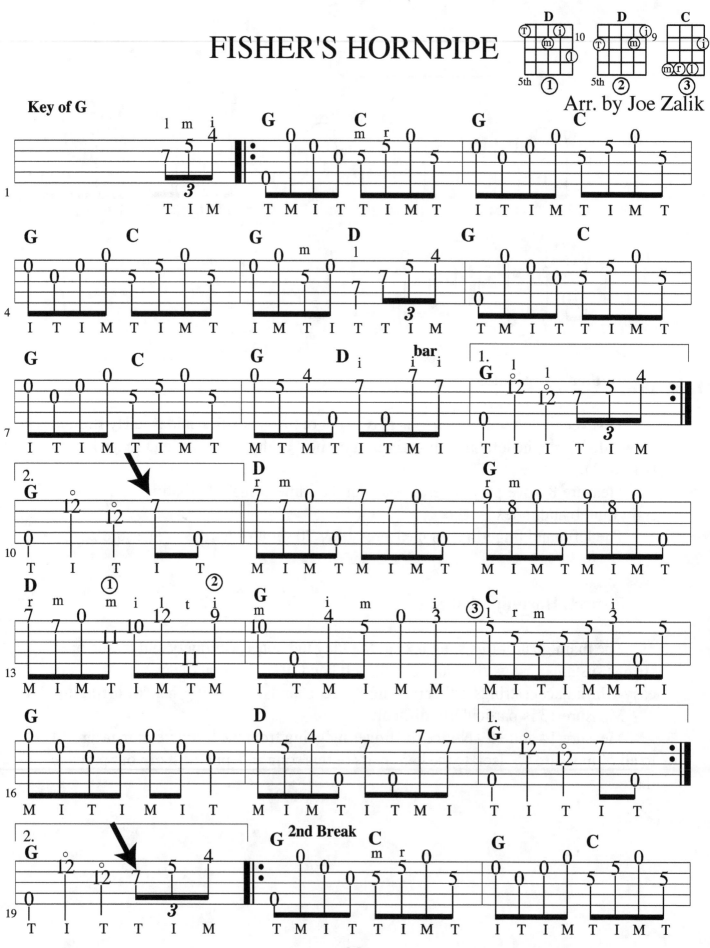

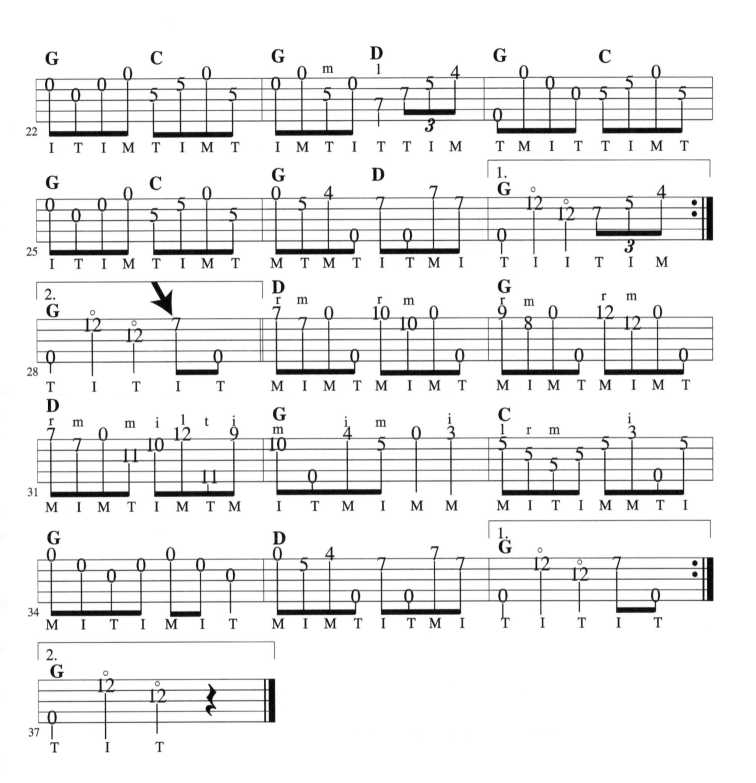

33

BLACK MOUNTAIN RAG

Arr. by Geoff Hohwald

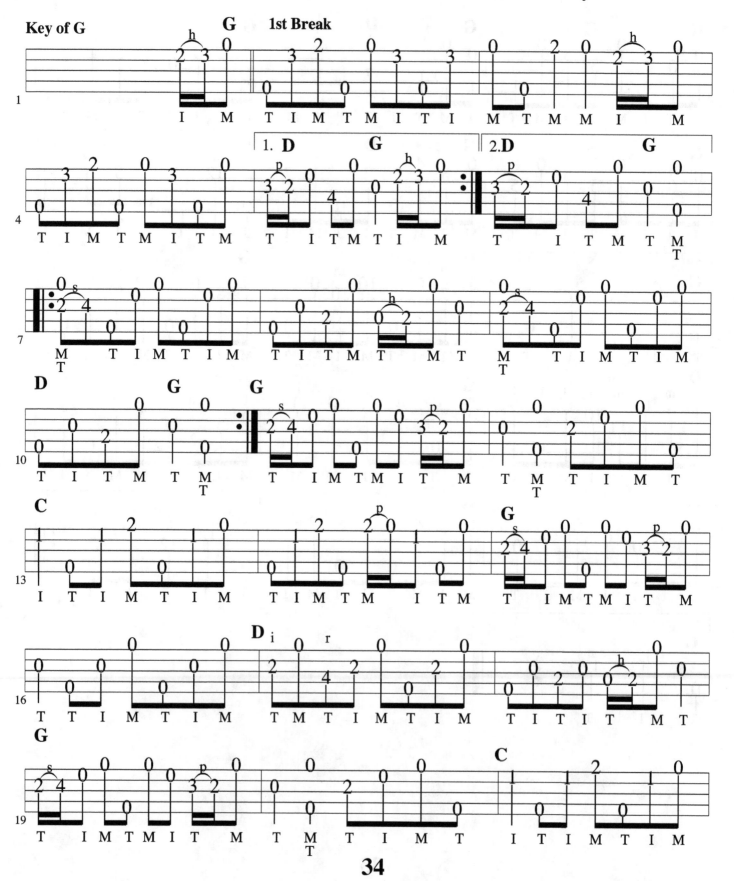

34

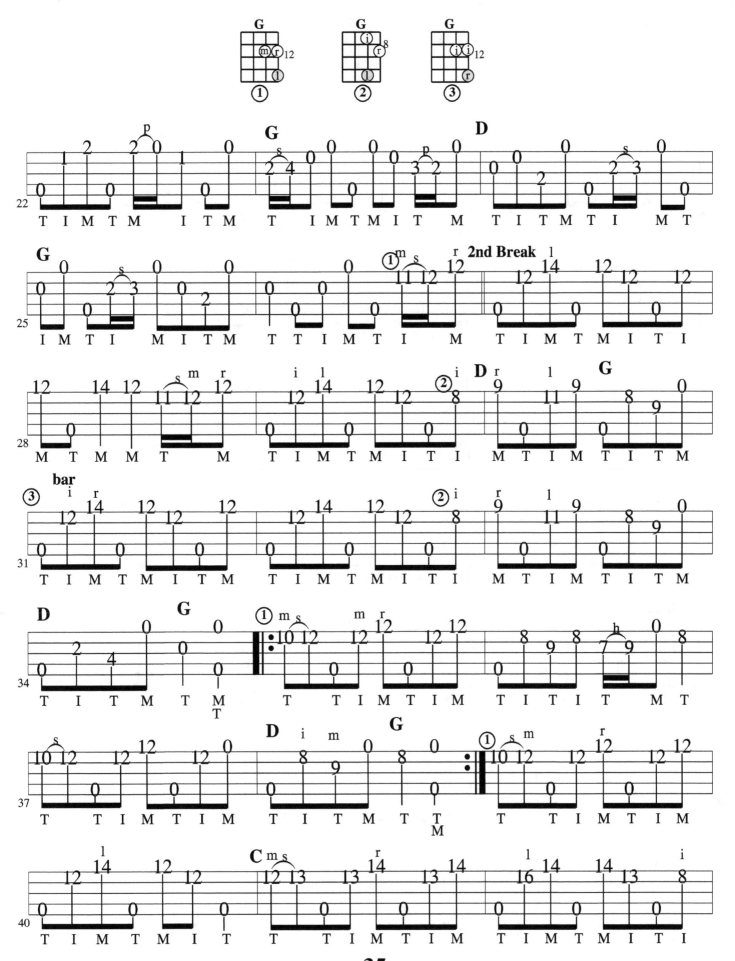

35

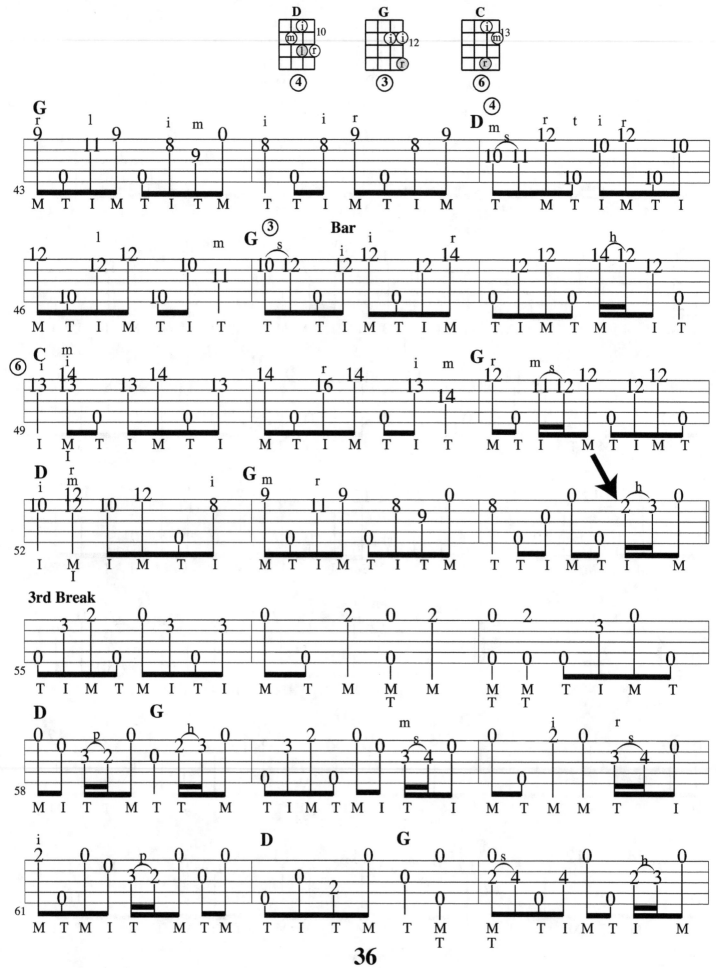

36

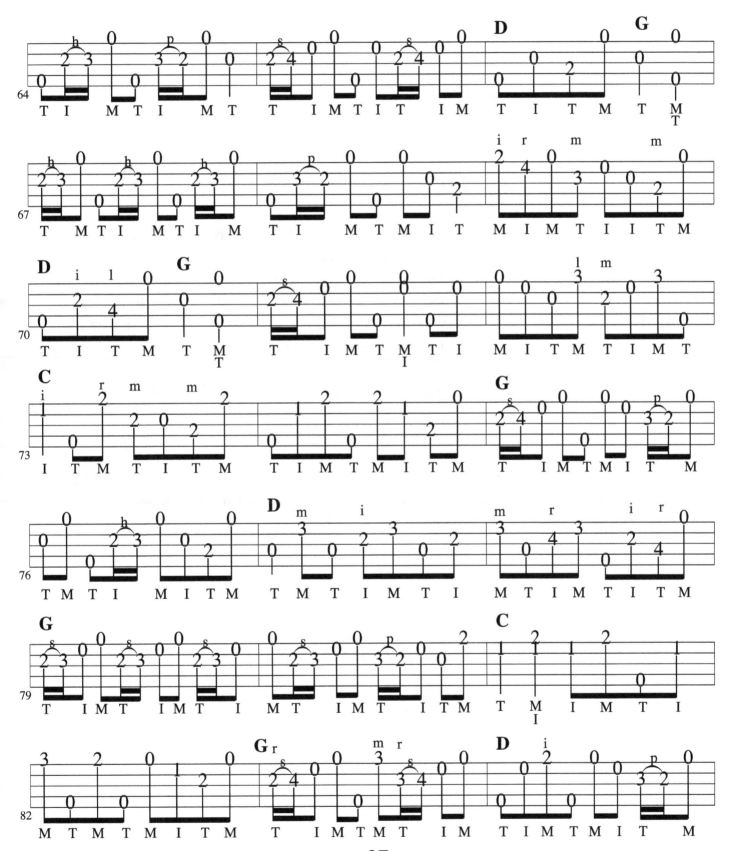

37

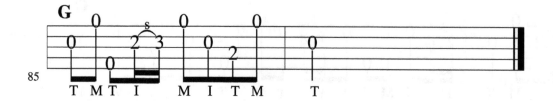

Black Mountain Rag Notes

This version of *Black Mountain Rag* contains a lot of percussive licks and these licks only sound good if played properly. To achieve this, remember that each lick represents different timing, techniques, or fingerings and should be isolated and practiced separately. Bear in mind that many of these licks took me months to perfect, so don't expect to be able to play them in 2 or 3 days. Measures to pay attention to are 14, 45-46, 51-52, 53-58, 59-61, 63-64, 65-66, 67-68, 71-73, and 83-85. Record yourself playing these licks and compare them with the Audio Tracks. We have played the slow versions at 43 bpm to emphasize the percussive quality of the licks.

Towards the end of the song, many of these licks are strung back to back, which is not typical. Don't be surprised when playing two difficult licks back to back, that you mess up the 2nd lick. The solution is to substitute rolls or an easier lick for the 2nd one. The other problem with stringing too many powerful licks together is that you overpower the listener. In conclusion, most banjo players will play the 1st Break as written and pick and choose licks from the 2nd & 3rd Breaks.

For access to the audio tracks for this course, go to this address on the web:

cvls.com/extras/banjosongs/

CUMBERLAND GAP

Arr. by Geoff Hohwald

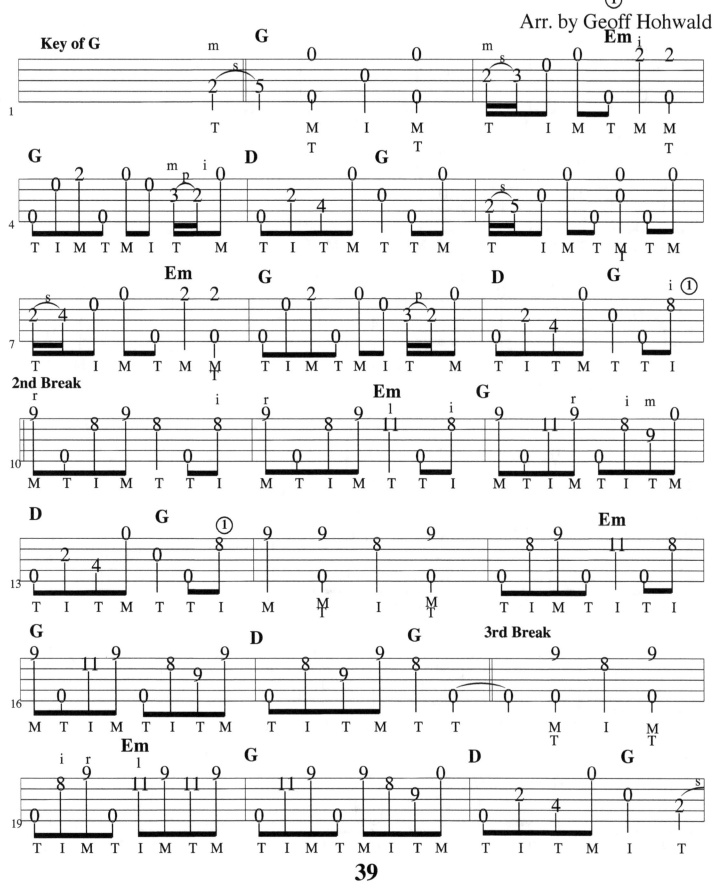

39

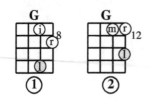

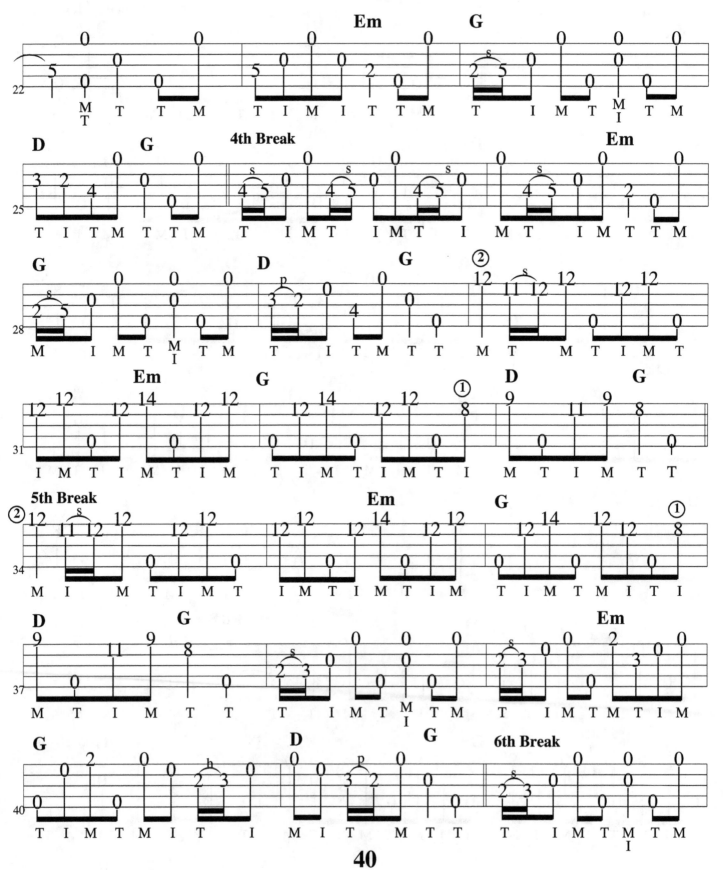

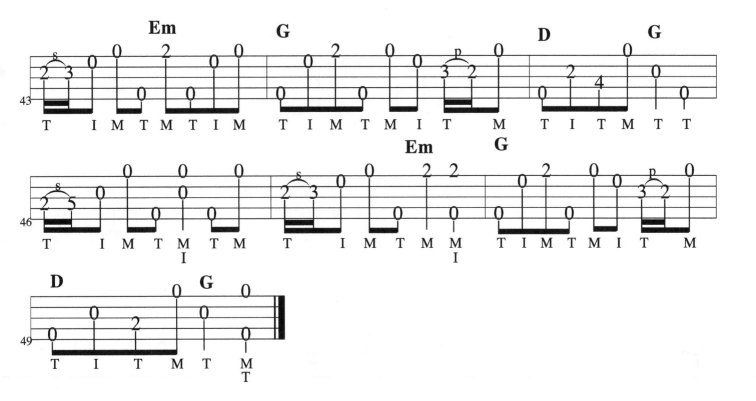

Cumberland Gap Notes

Because this song repeats itself every four measures, we include lots of variations of simple licks to make the song more interesting. Compare measures 2-5 with measures 6-9. Also, compare measures 10-13 to 14-17. Watch the fingering, get the timing correct, and listen to the Audio Tracks.

John Hardy Notes

The first 2 breaks of *John Hardy* are fairly straight forward. Notice the left hand fingerings are used in a lot of other songs in this book and work best for most people. The D shape (little finger on 1st string @ 4th fret, middle finger on 2nd string @ 3rd fret, index finger on 3rd string @ 2nd fret) is held from the 14th measure through measure 18. The 3rd Break is a Billy McKinley arrangement. Measures 54 -61 are unusual and will require a lot of practice. Because this break goes off into space, it'll throw off any guitar player that's not paying attention to the timing. This break, if executed properly, will amaze your friends and family.

JOHN HARDY

Arr. by Hohwald & McKinley

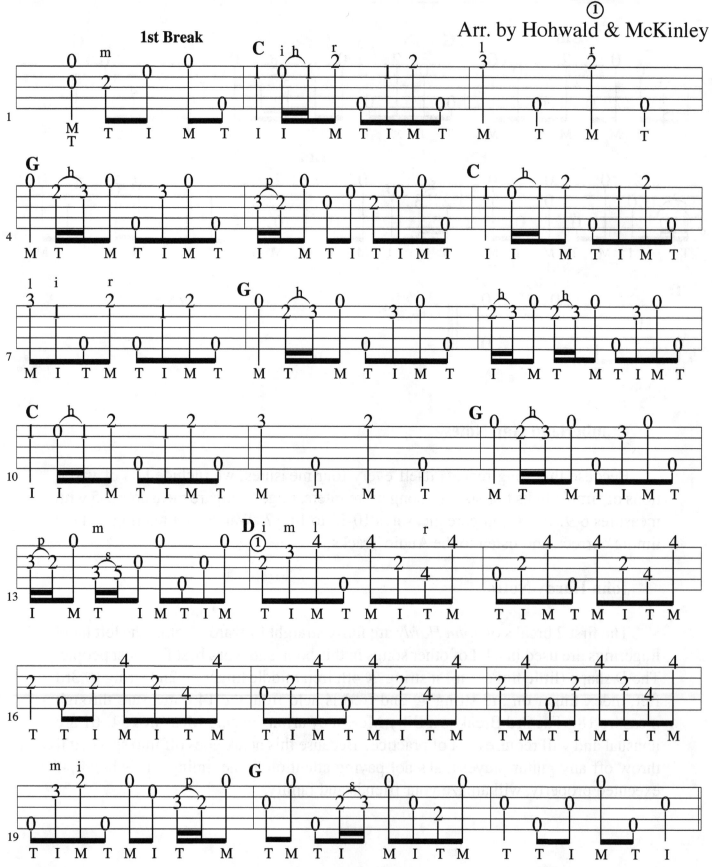

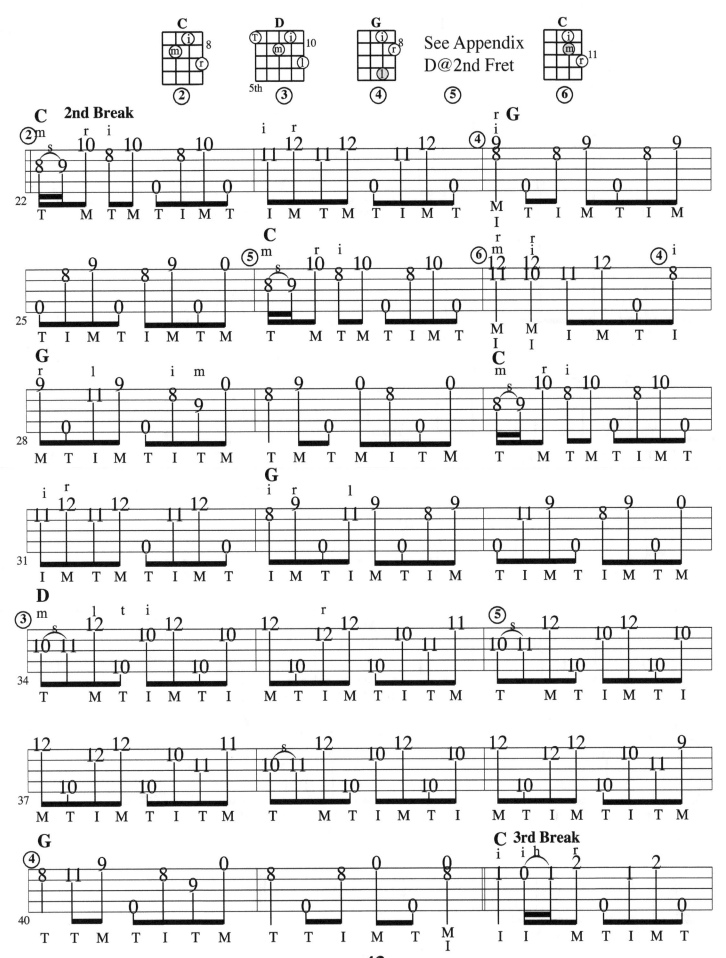

43

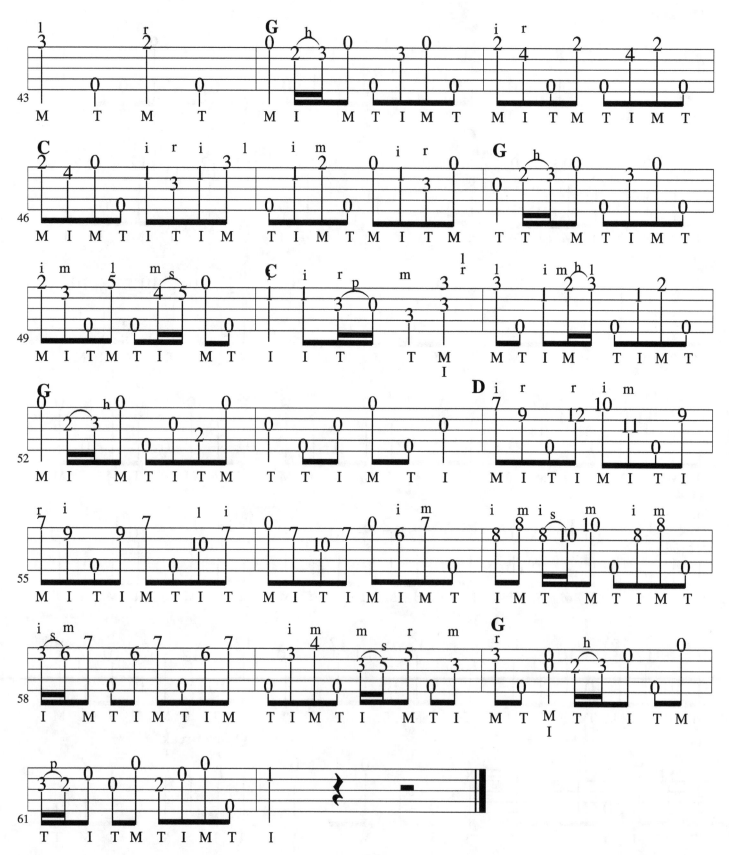

44

IN THE PINES

Arr. by Geoff Hohwald

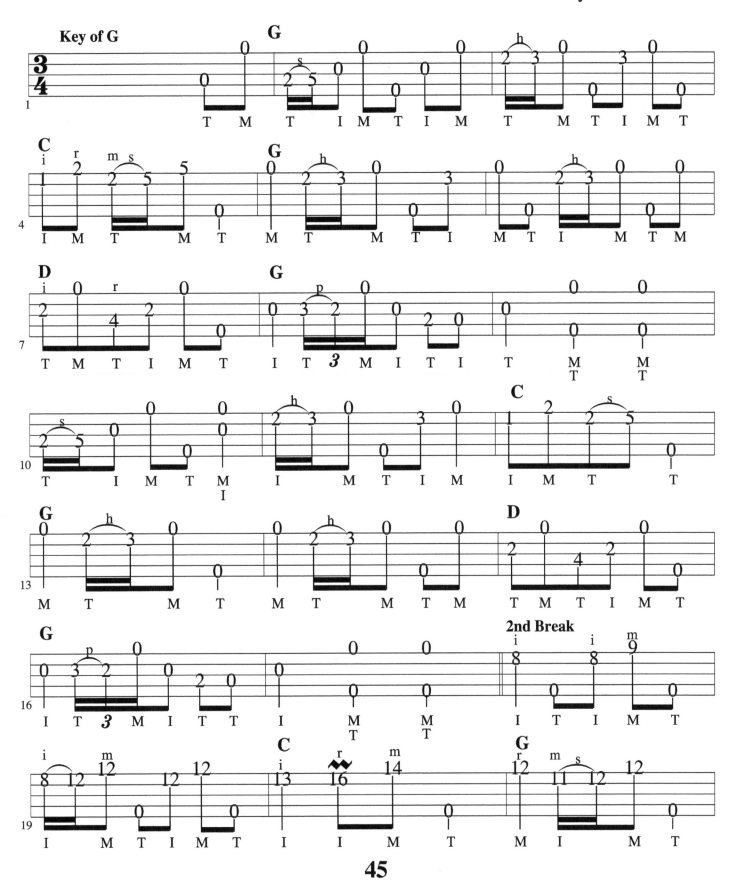

45

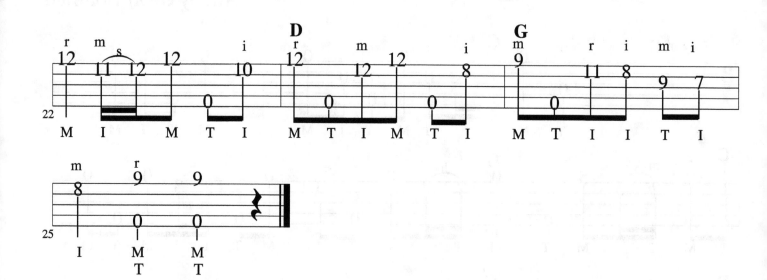

In The Pines Notes

This song is played in 3/4 or waltz time. It includes triplets. Work on timing and clarity by listening to the Audio Tracks.

For access to the audio tracks for this course, go to this address on the web:

cvls.com/extras/banjosongs/

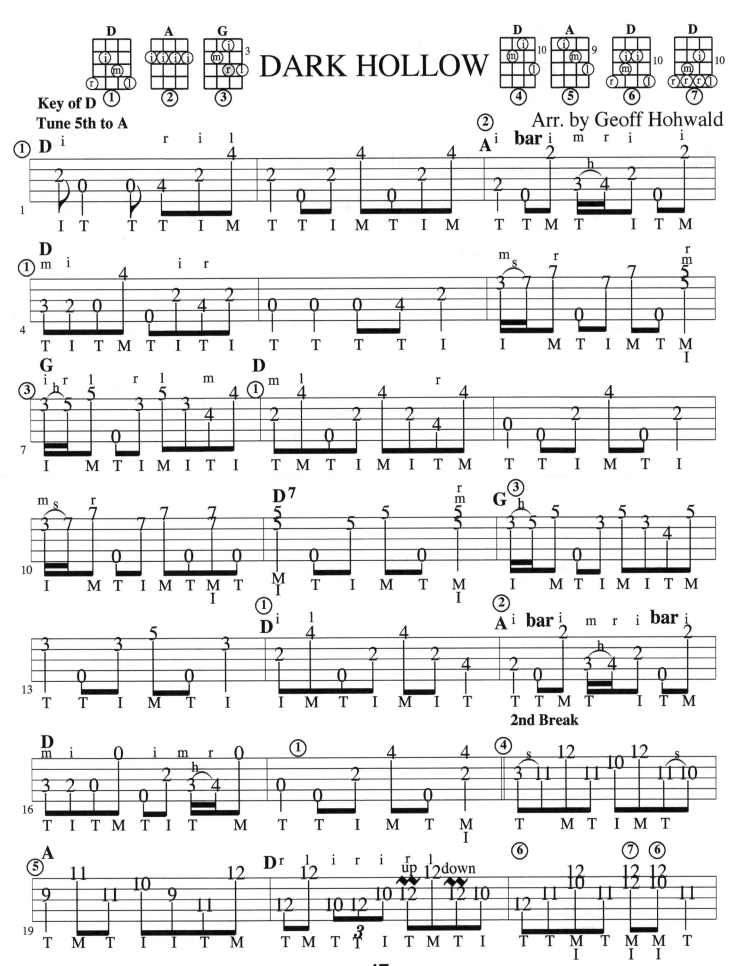

DARK HOLLOW

Arr. by Geoff Hohwald

Key of D
Tune 5th to A

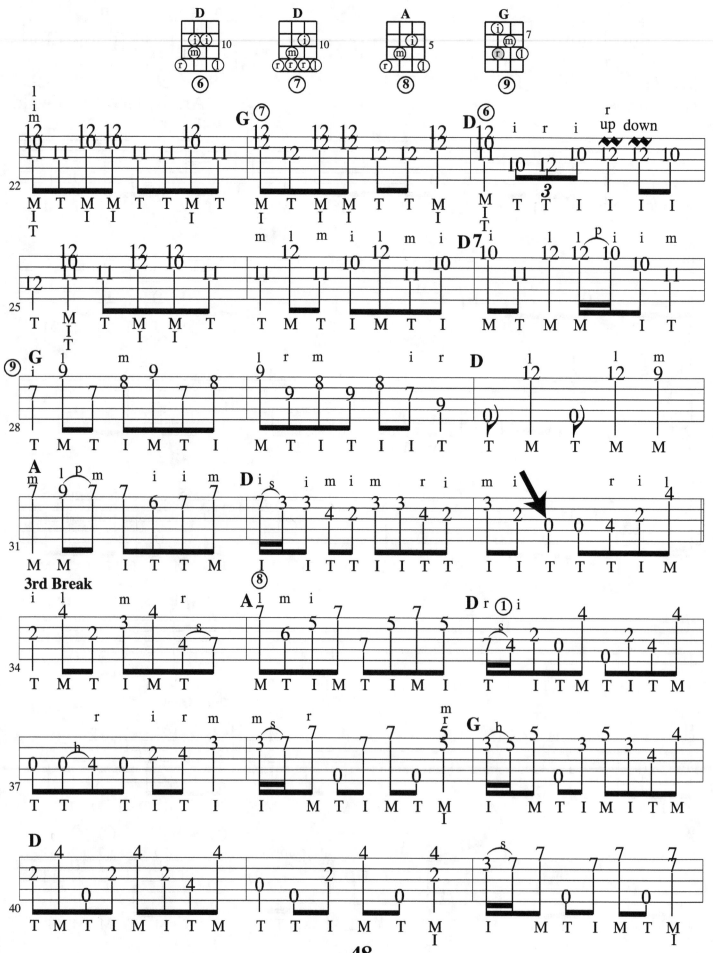

48

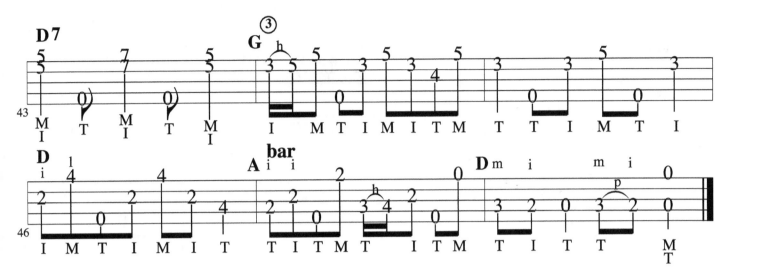

Dark Hollow Notes

Dark Hollow is played in the Key of D. The different chord forms are noted on the top of the page. Pay special attention to transitions (going from one chord position to another or moving the same position up and down the neck). Study the transitions between measures 2 and 3, 7 and 8, 18 and 19, 35 and 36. Also, review the Appendix, page 106, moving the C shape when doing a slide.

Once you have mastered these movements in one song, they can be transferred to others.

DIXIE

Arr. by Geoff Hohwald

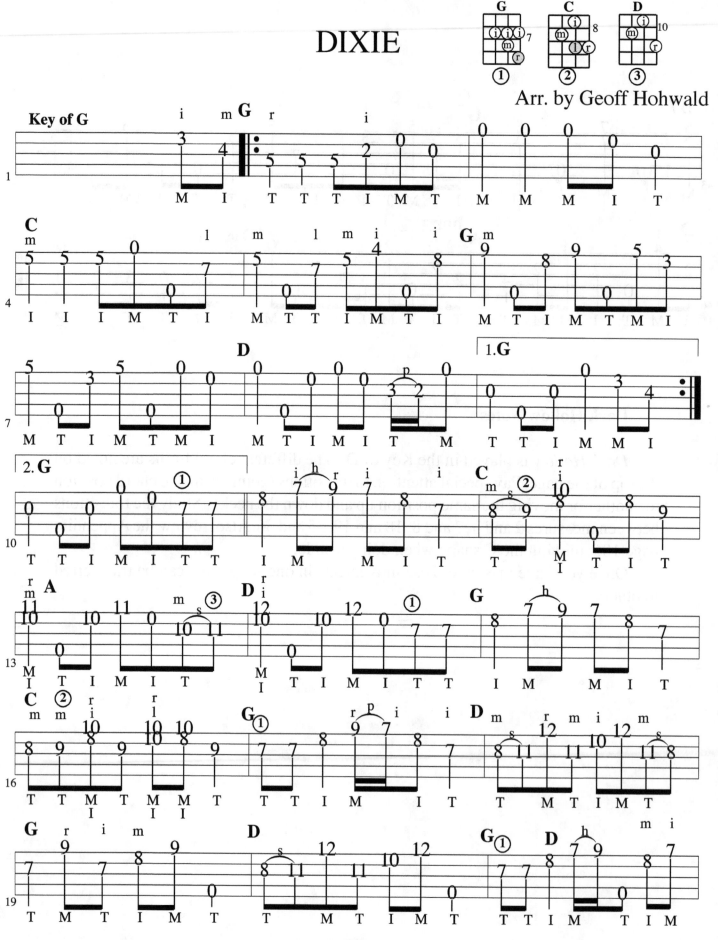

50

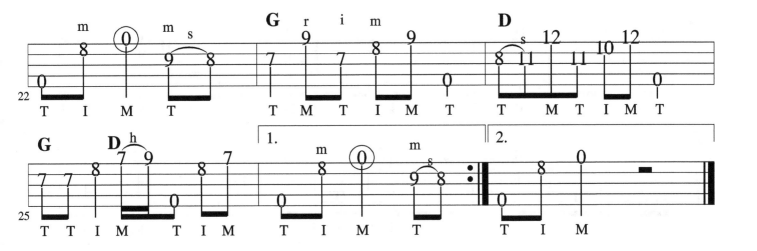

Dixie Notes

Dixie contains a lot of left hand movement. To assist you, there are several diagrams included. Additional left hand forms can be figured out by looking at the fingering above the measures. When the first note of a sequence is played, the complete chord form is placed on the fretboard. Measures 12, 13, 14, 16, 18, 19, 20, 23, & 24 are examples of this.

Boil Them Cabbage Down Notes

This arrangement is fairly easy and can be used for either lead or back up. The left hand fingering is very simple. You will notice that the right hand plays a continuous roll during measures 17 - 24 and measures 25 - 31. This is a great way to see how a forward roll can be used. If you have the *Banjo Primer* book, you can get additional variations to this song.

We played the slow breaks at 43 bpm to give you the opportunity to focus on the individual notes and rolls.

BOIL THEM CABBAGE DOWN

Arr. by Geoff Hohwald

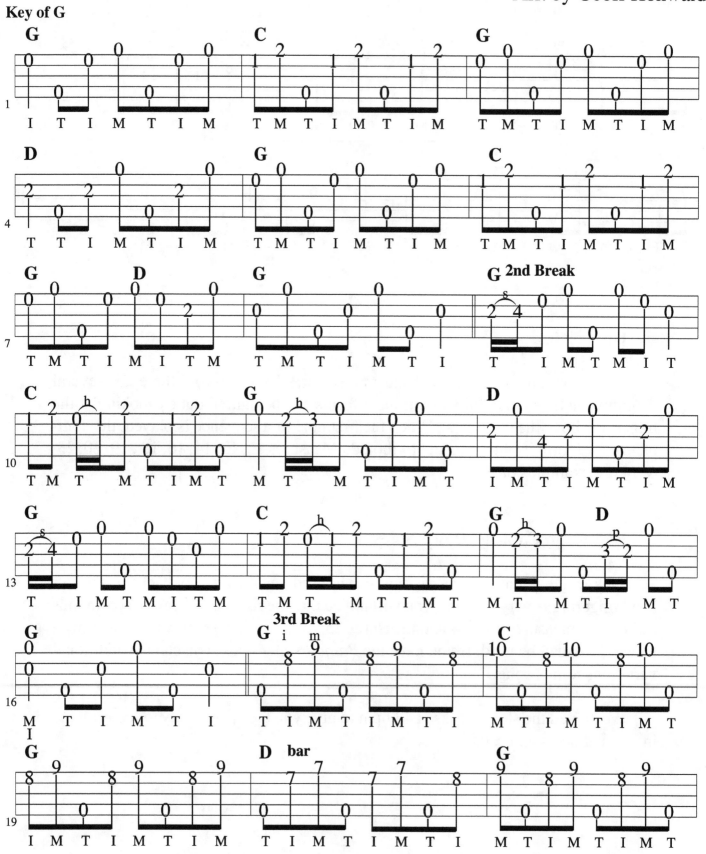

52

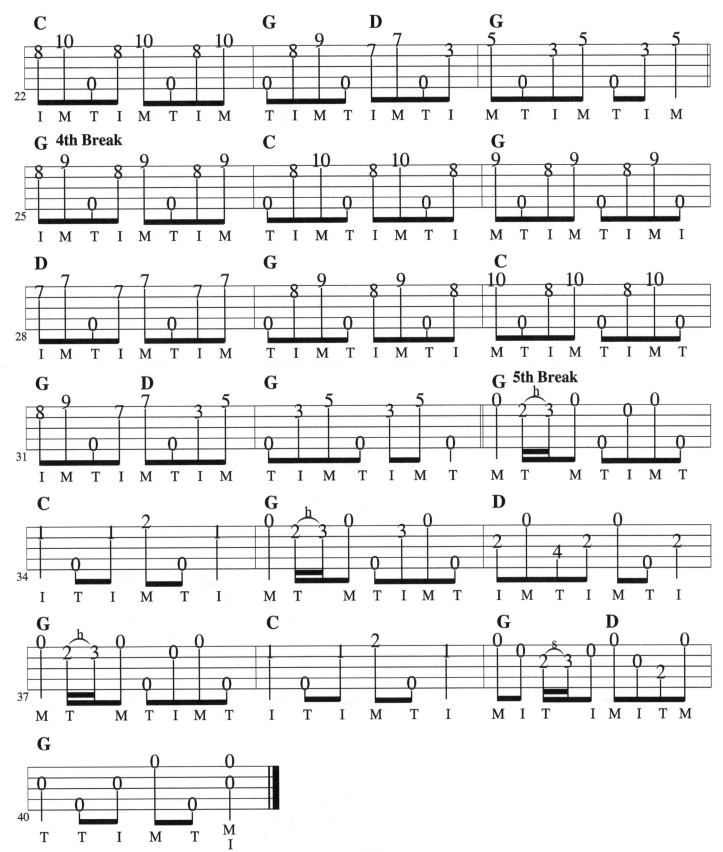

LITTLE MAGGIE

Arr. by Geoff Hohwald

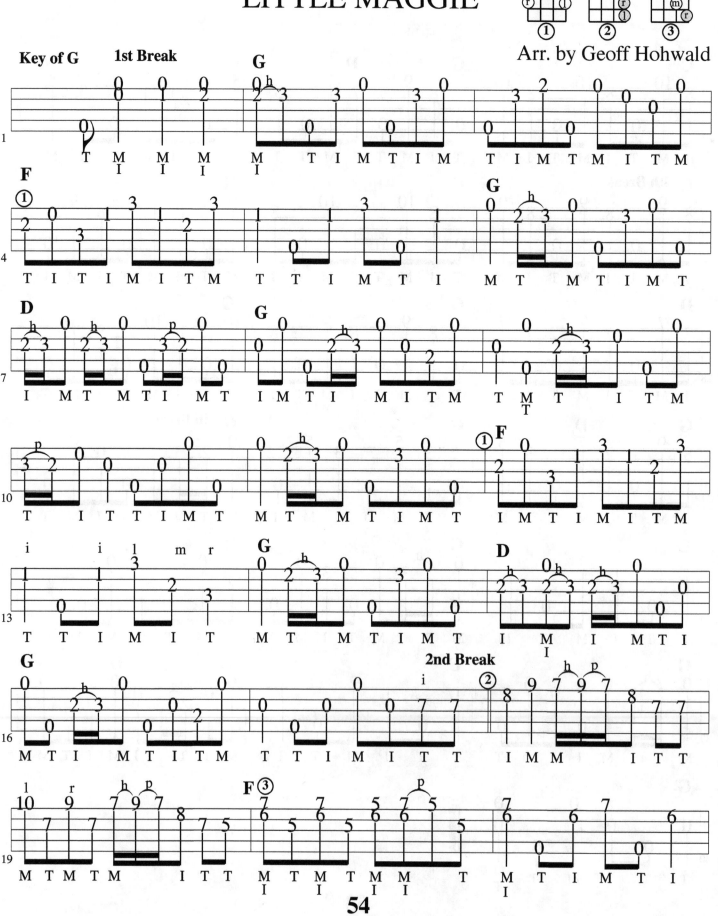

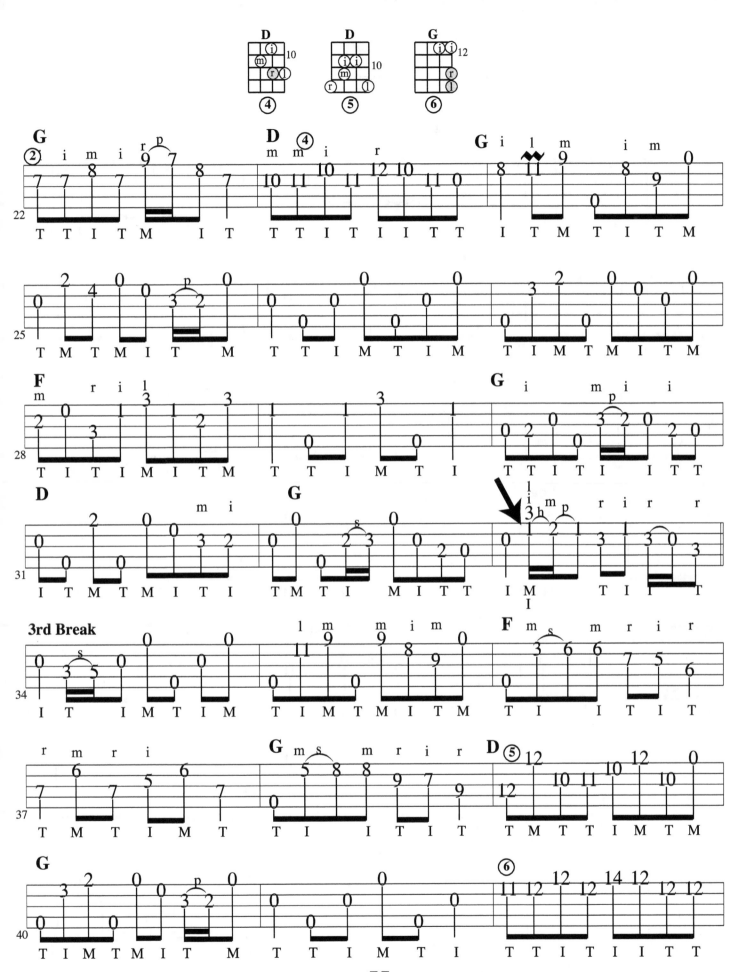

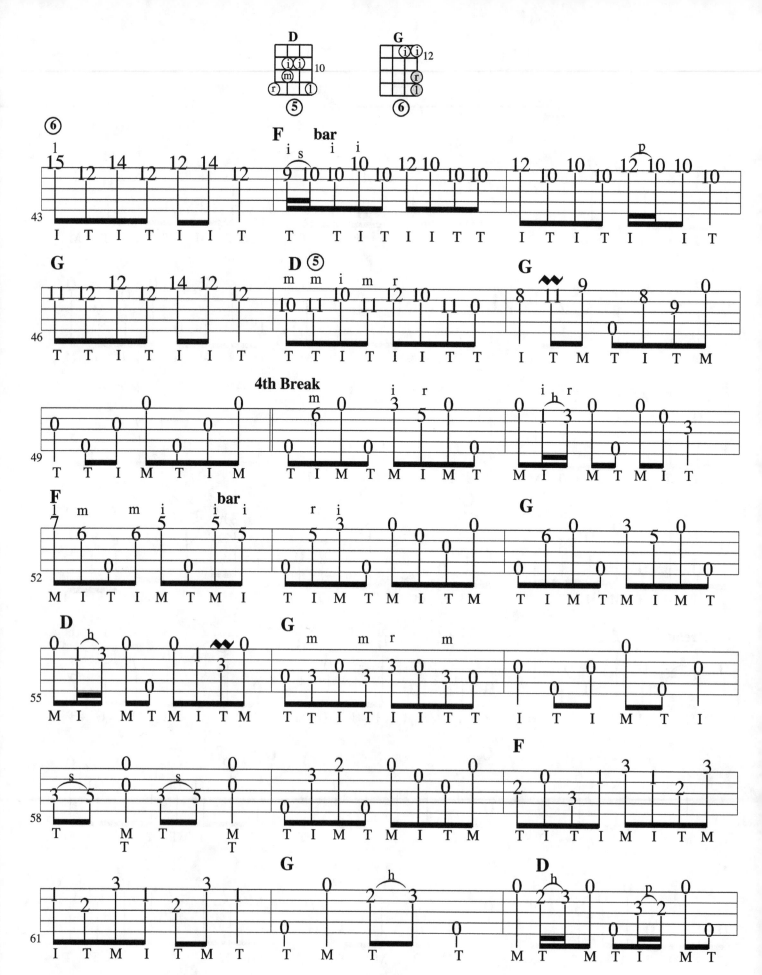

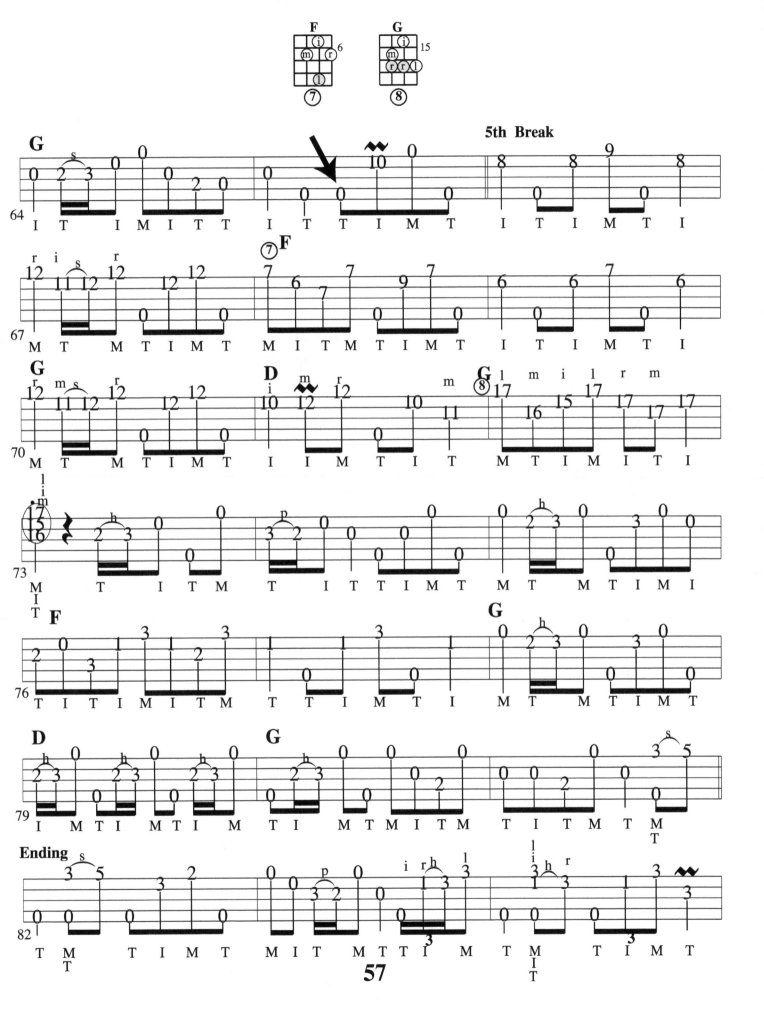

57

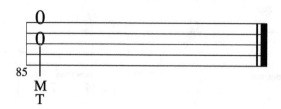

85

M
T

Little Maggie Notes

Little Maggie consists of 4 breaks, which contain several distinct techniques or styles. Not only can these be used in *Little Maggie*, but they can be pulled out of context and used in other songs.

Measures 17-22 - Watch the left and right hand fingerings and listen carefully to the Audio Tracks. You will see a similar technique in *Dixie*, measures 10-11 and 15.

Measures 23 and 33 - Practice these measures individually.

Measures 36-37 - Practice the slide from the 3rd to the 6th fret until it sounds like the Audio Tracks. This is a lick frequently used in back up.

Measure 38 is similar to measure 36, but is transposed from F to G.

Measure 39 - A classic backup lick that can be transposed easily.

Measures 42-46 - Another back up technique that is heard on a lot of slow songs. The index finger bars the 1st and 2nd strings and holds this position through measures 42 and 43.

Measure 44 - The index finger bars the 1st and 2nd strings at the 10th fret and holds it until measure 46.

Measures 50-51 - Interesting blues chromatic lick.

Measures 52-53 - The rest of the lick starting on 50-51

Measures 60-61 - Listen to the accent.

Measures 71-72 - This is one of my favorite licks. To be effective, it must be played very clearly. By breaking down each song into its component parts and concentrating on them, your playing will improve, particularly with left hand fingering up the neck. You will also be able to analyze other songs and make them clearer and better sounding.

PALLET ON YOUR FLOOR

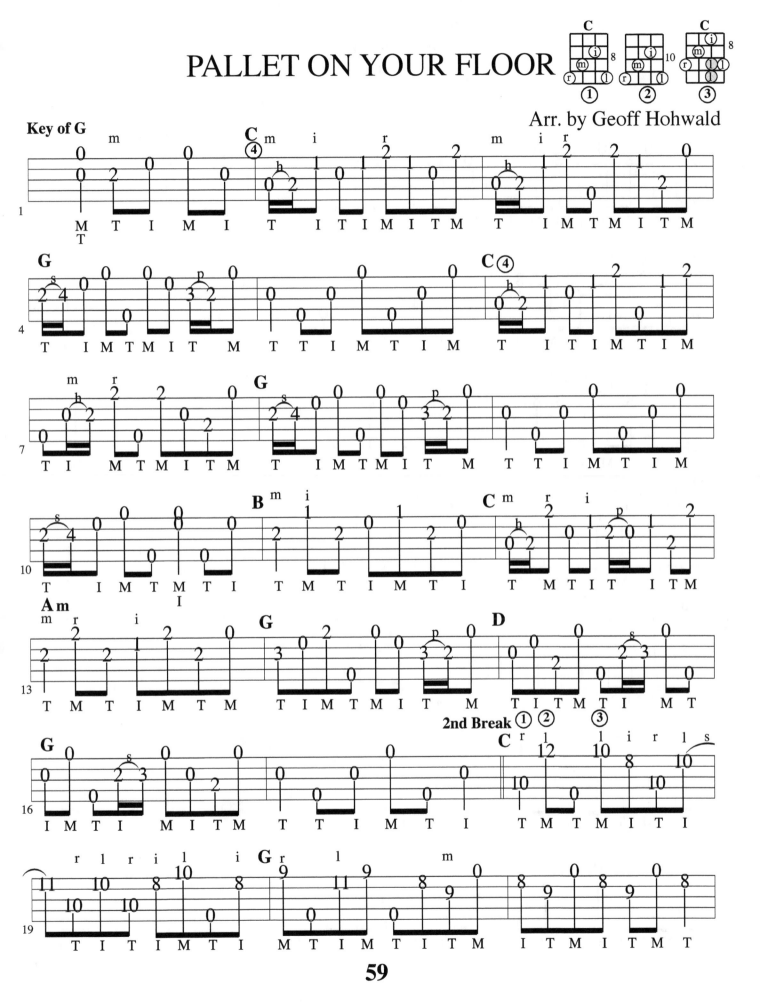

Arr. by Geoff Hohwald

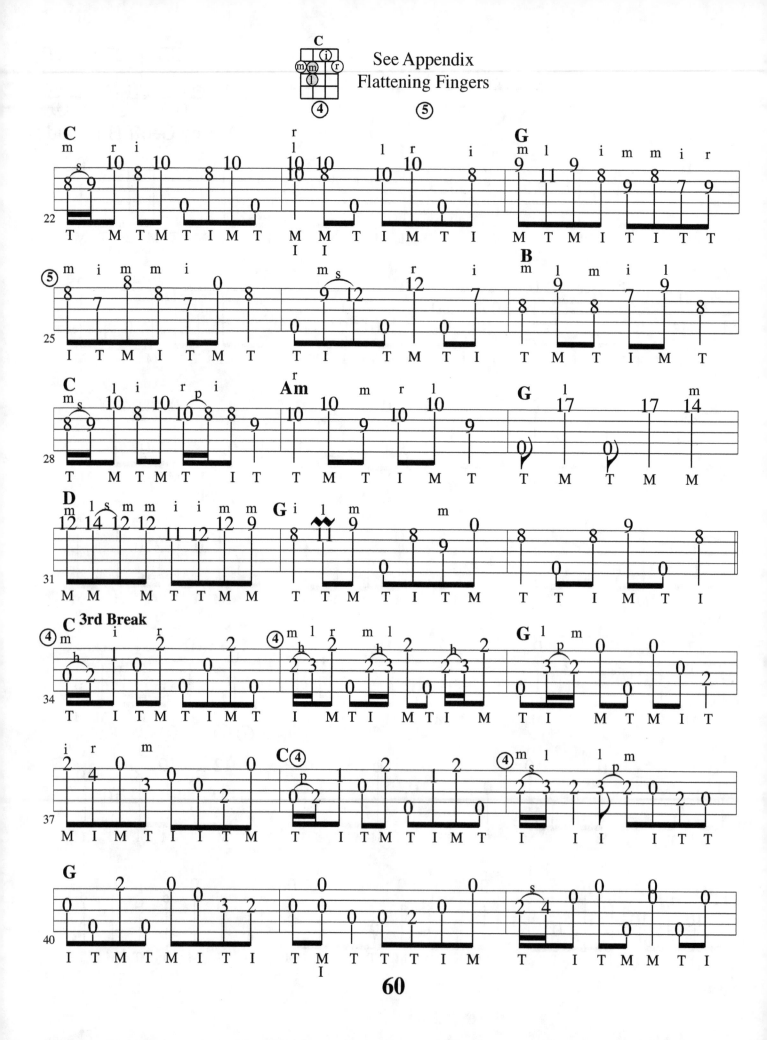

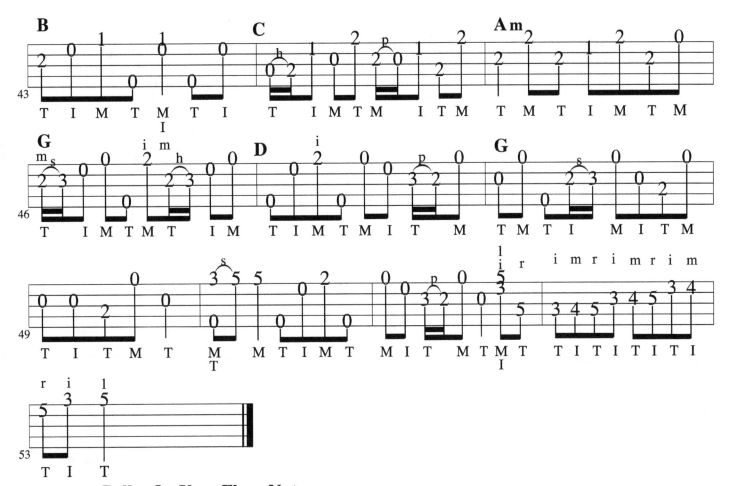

Pallet On Your Floor Notes

Pallet On Your Floor is an exercise in left hand movement. Look at the left hand fingerings, the chord diagrams, and the following measures:

Measure 13 - While holding the C Shape with the left hand, the left middle finger moves from the 4th string 2nd fret to the 3rd string 2nd fret to become an Am chord.

Measure 24 - The left hand fingering is correct. Listen carefully to the Audio Tracks.

Measure 27 - This is essentially the C Shape mentioned above, but moved back one fret. Study the left hand fingerings to find the shape.

Measure 28 - The same shape as measure 27 moved up one fret.

Measure 29 - Leave the same fingers down as in measure 28 and add the left ring finger at the 10th fret and it becomes an Am shape.

It takes a lot of extra time to identify the left hand movements for up the neck breaks, but it makes them possible to play cleanly and with speed. As you go through these notes and analyze the fingerings, you will become better at it and be able to apply your knowledge to other songs. **61**

WHEN THE SAINTS GO MARCHING IN

Arr. by Geoff Hohwald

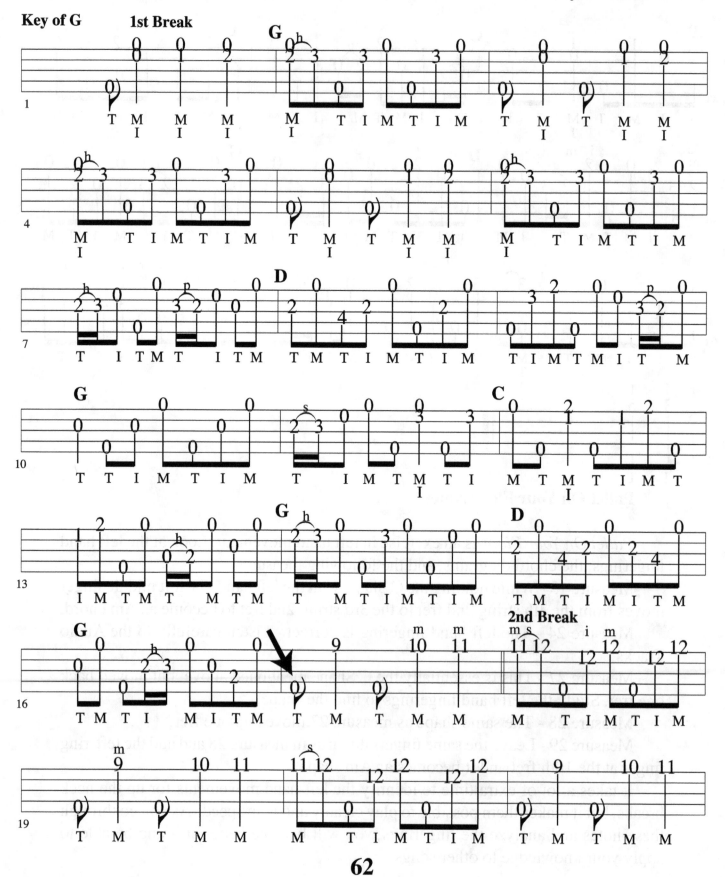

62

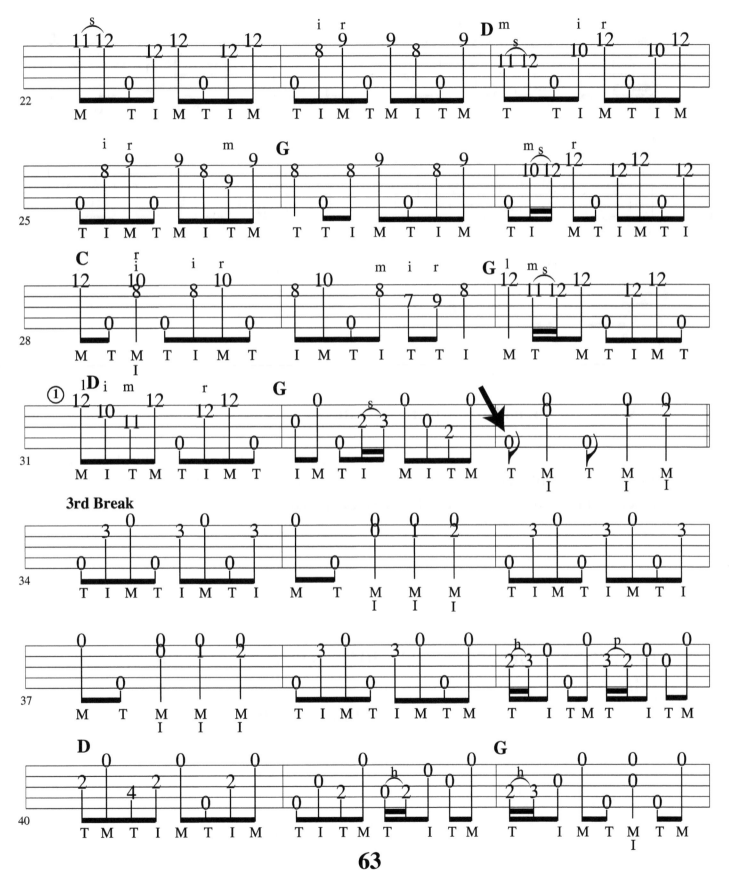

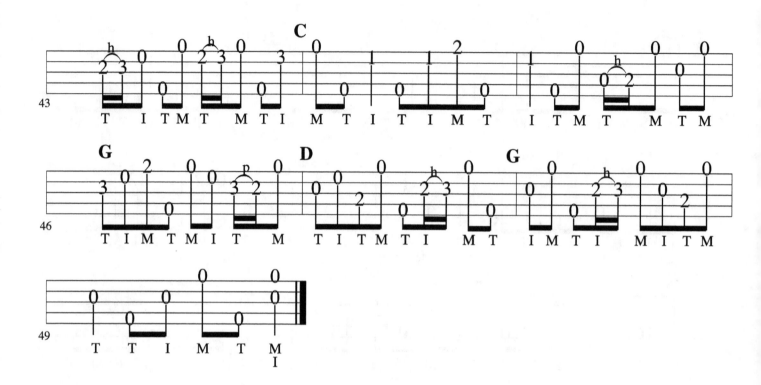

When The Saints Go Marching In Notes

When The Saints Go Marching In is included as a song that people not familiar with bluegrass will recognize. Many times you will be asked to play your banjo for friends and relatives. This song is fairly self explanatory.

For access to the audio tracks for this course, go to this address on the web:

cvls.com/extras/banjosongs/

RED HAIRED BOY

Arr. by Hohwald & McKinley

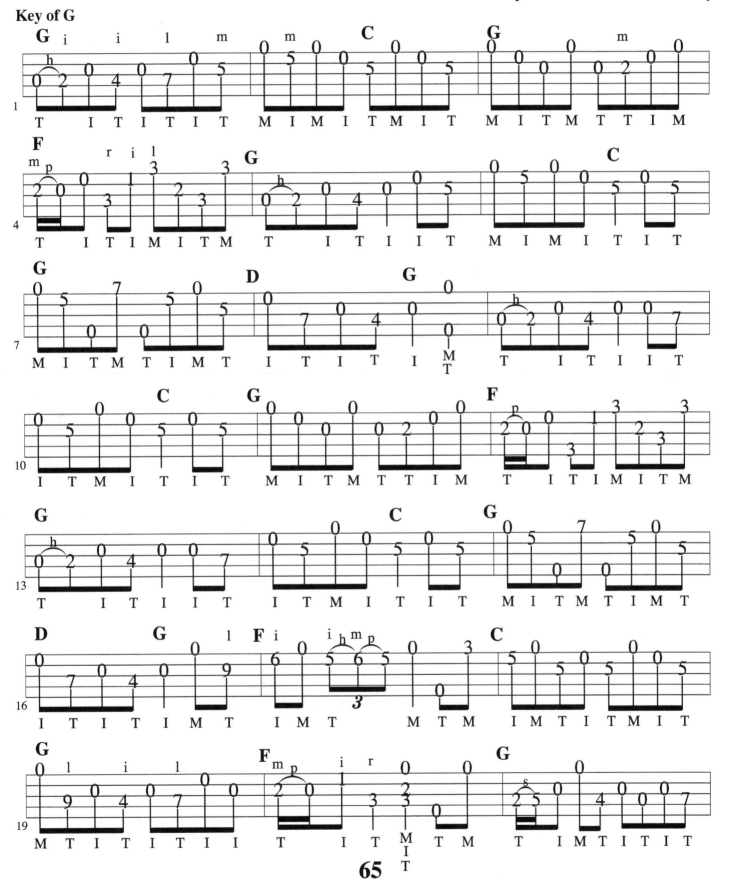

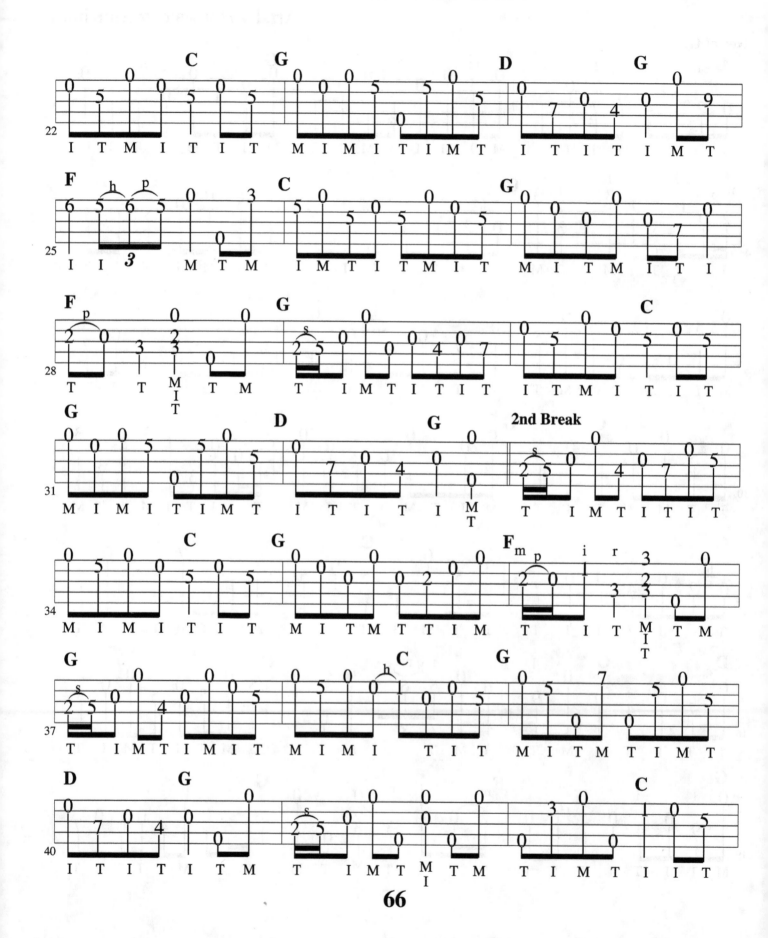

66

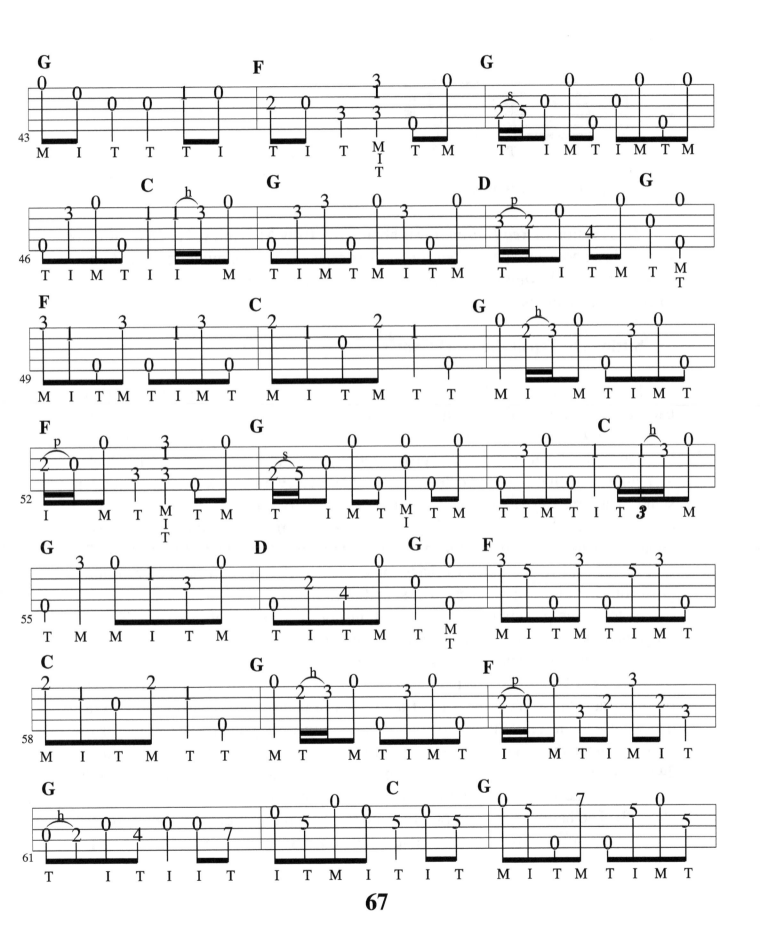

67

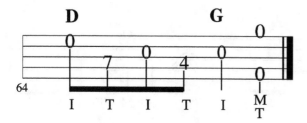

Red Haired Boy Notes

This version of *Red Haired Boy* is about 70% Billy McKinley. This song sounds good at just about any speed. *Red Haired Boy* repeats a lot of similar licks and fingerings. If you are having trouble with a certain passage, go back to a similar passage to get the left hand fingerings.

Sitting On Top of the World Notes

It took about 10 days to write this arrangement. I was visiting my relatives and had little to do, so I pulled out a banjo that I keep at my mother's house and started working on it. I had no tab paper, so I took some flyers that my sister had and drew lines on the back with a pencil and proceeded to write out this arrangement. I wanted to include licks that communicated rhythm and power, which took me years to understand. The first 15 years I played, I would occasionally run into a player at a festival or jam session whose playing and licks had a feel that my playing did not have. After about 20 years, I started to be able to duplicate some of this feel. In *Sittin On Top Of The World*, I've attempted to share some of this. If you get lucky and run into a powerful rhythm guitarist, these will sound even better.

Note: Some players use an Em chord during the last part of this song. This arrangement is like the original version without the Em.

The correct left hand fingering is written above the music and should be studied. Measure 17, 18, 19 - This is a lick that is added after a break. If you are playing with rhythm tracks, it won't fit because it adds 3 extra measures. Measure 22 - Notice that we use the left little finger to note the 1st string 14th fret. The little finger is the weakest finger and will require extra attention to strengthen it. Measure 26 & measure 24 are the same. Measure 31 - The 6th note is somewhat unusual. You can play the 1st string at the 12 fret instead of doing the backwards slide. Measure 58 - Look at chord 3. The hammer ons and pull offs are done with the middle and little fingers. This is very difficult, but can be used as an exercise to strengthen the little finger.

SITTING ON TOP OF THE WORLD

Arr. by Geoff Hohwald

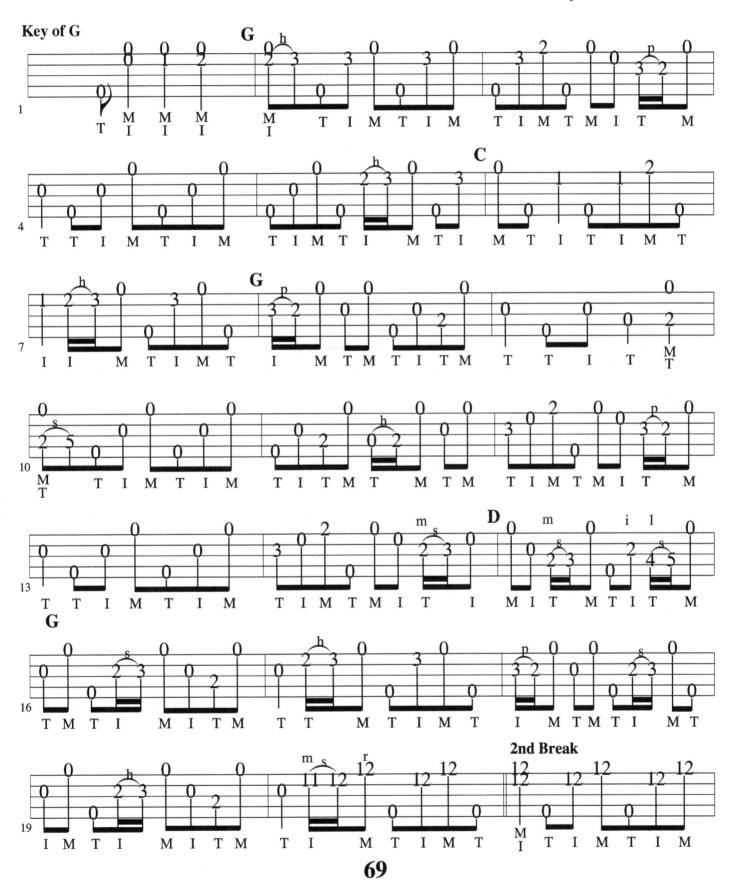

69

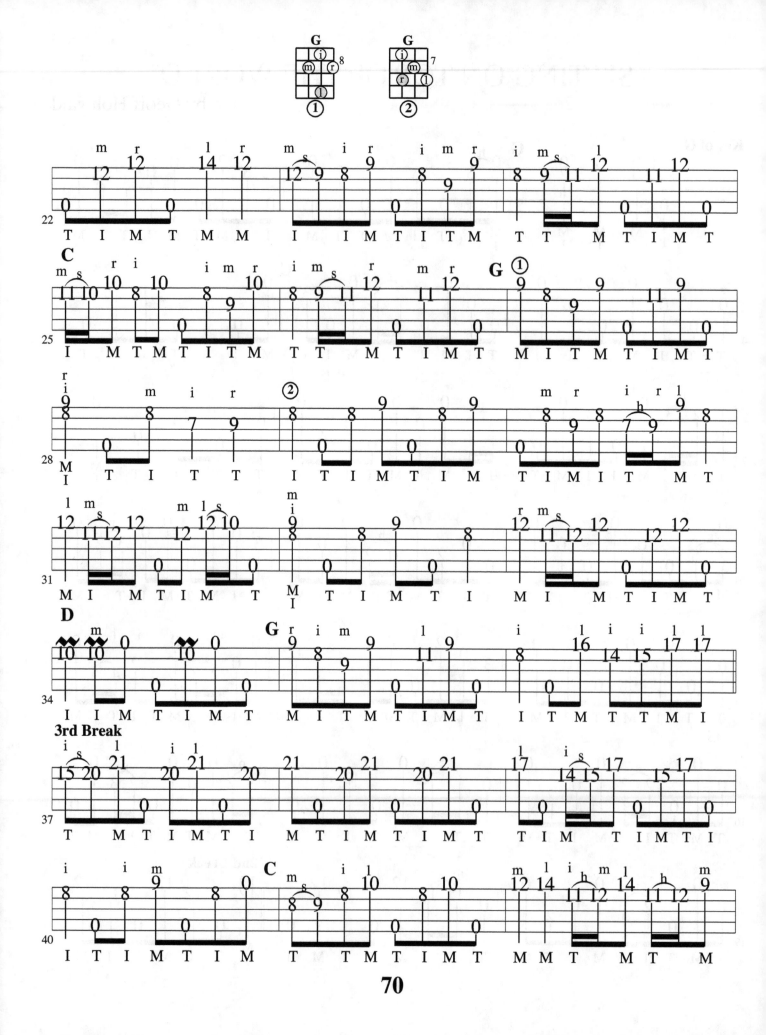

70

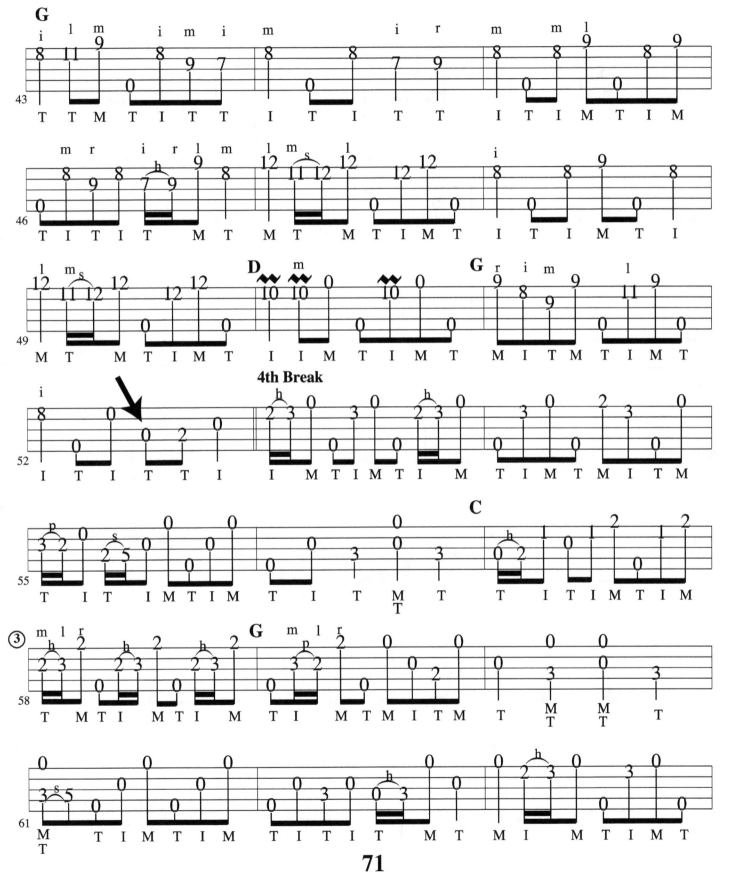

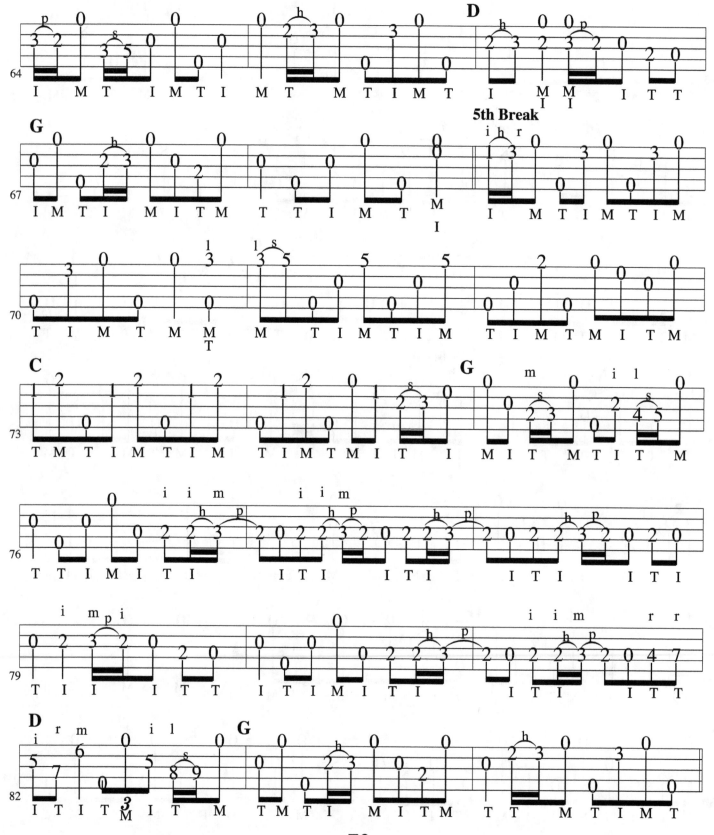

6th Break

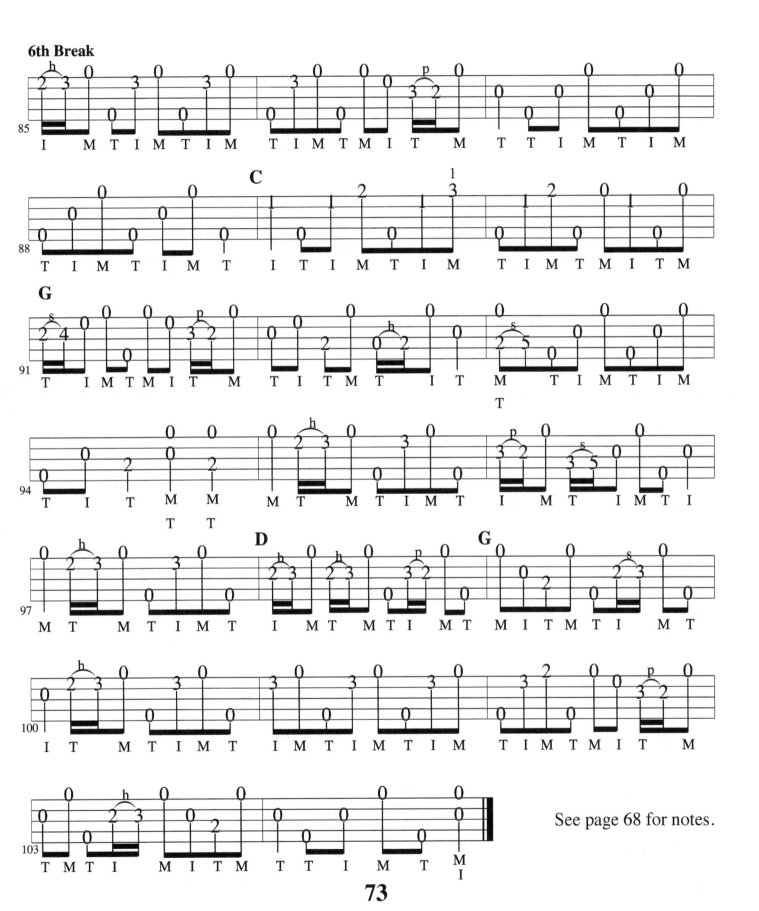

See page 68 for notes.

73

GRANDFATHER'S CLOCK

Arr. by Geoff Hohwald

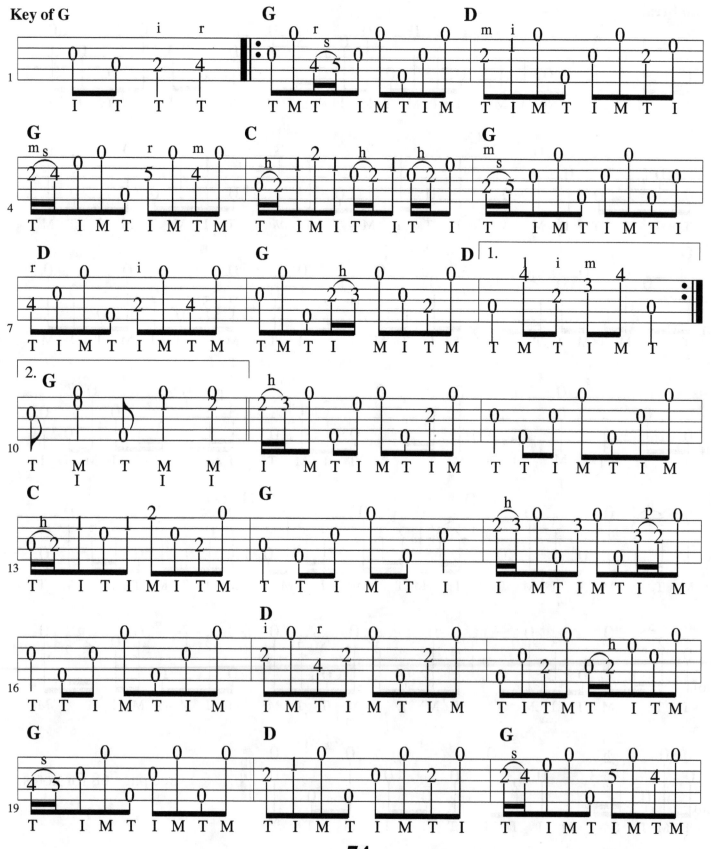

74

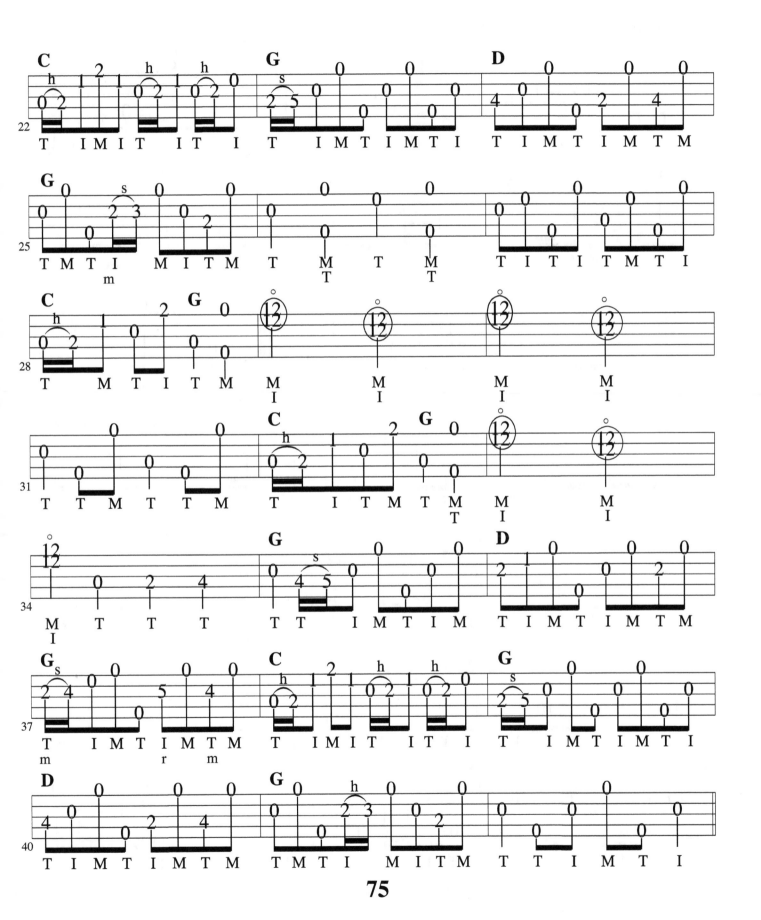

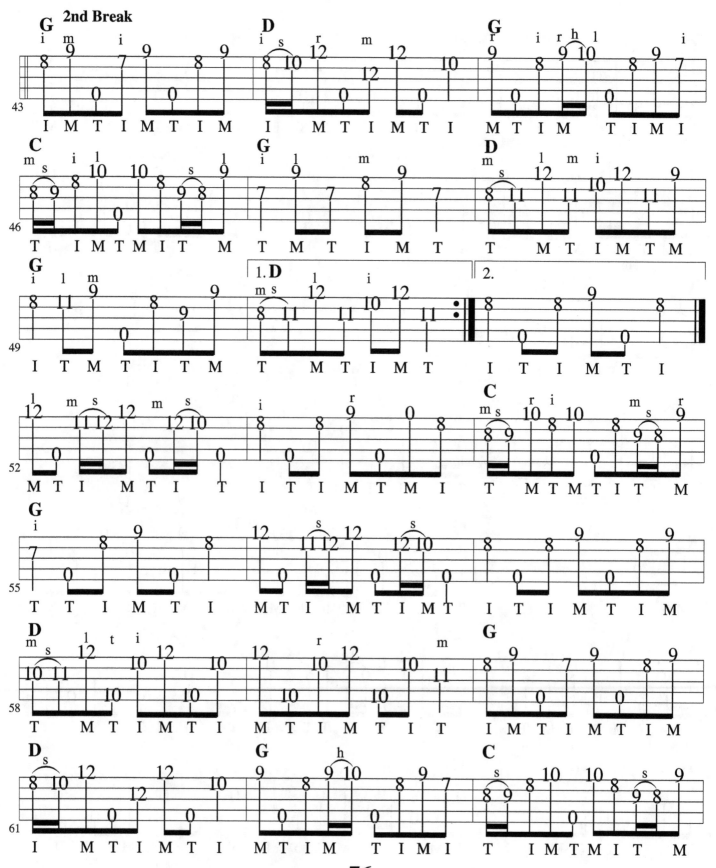

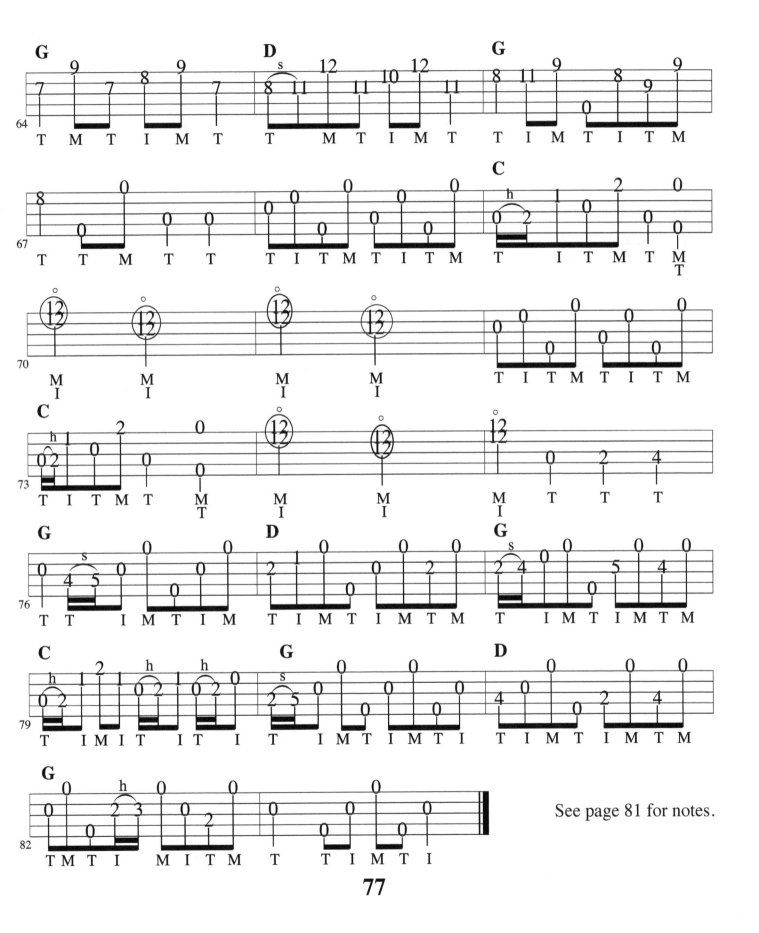

See page 81 for notes.

77

ROLL ON BUDDY

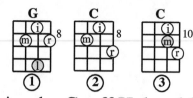

Arr. by Geoff Hohwald

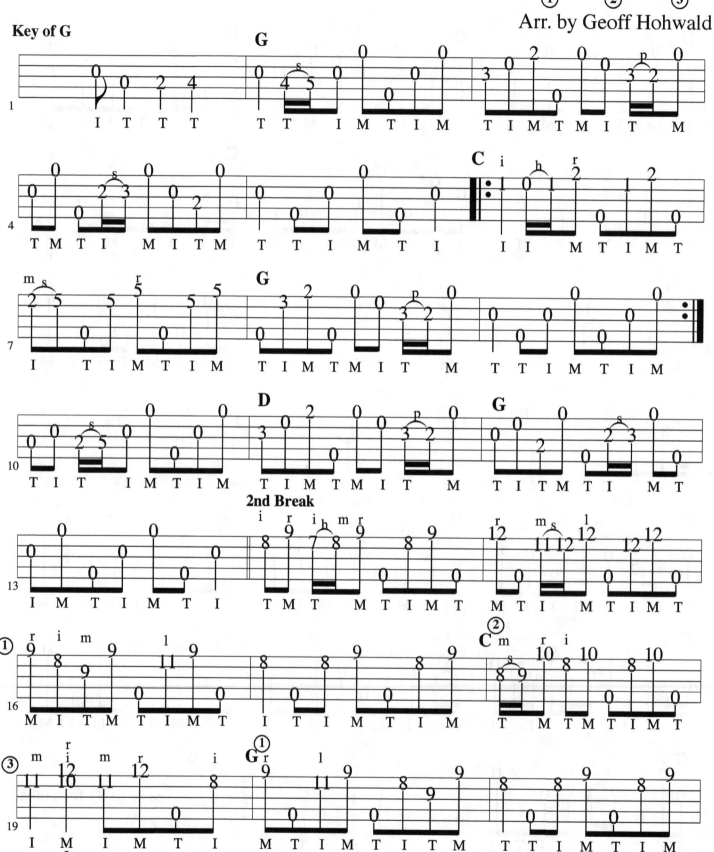

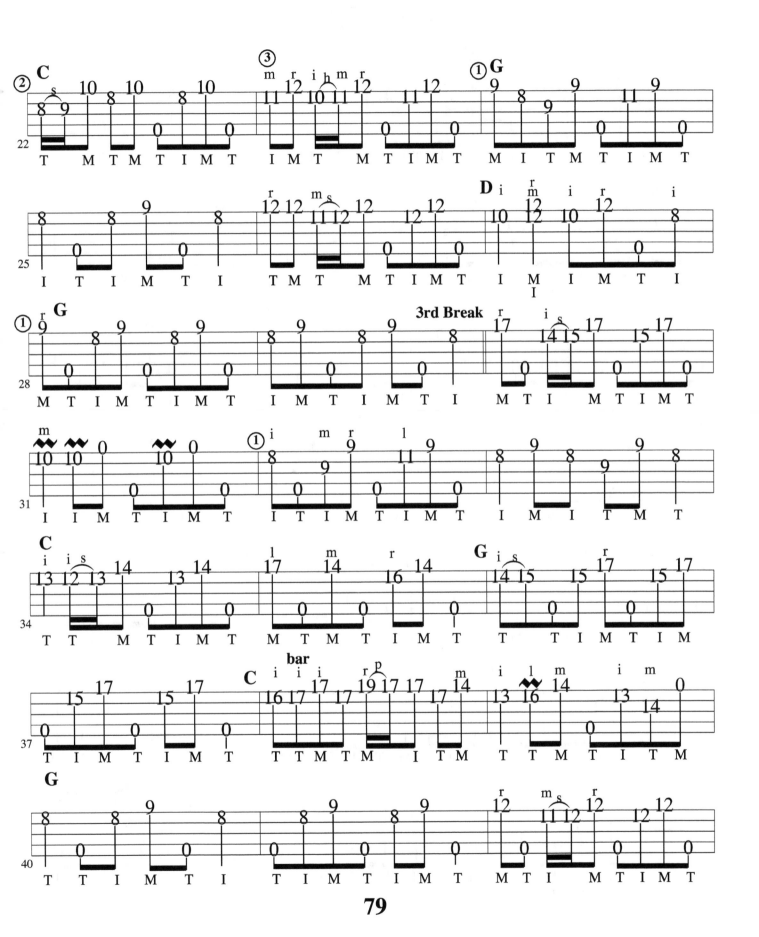

79

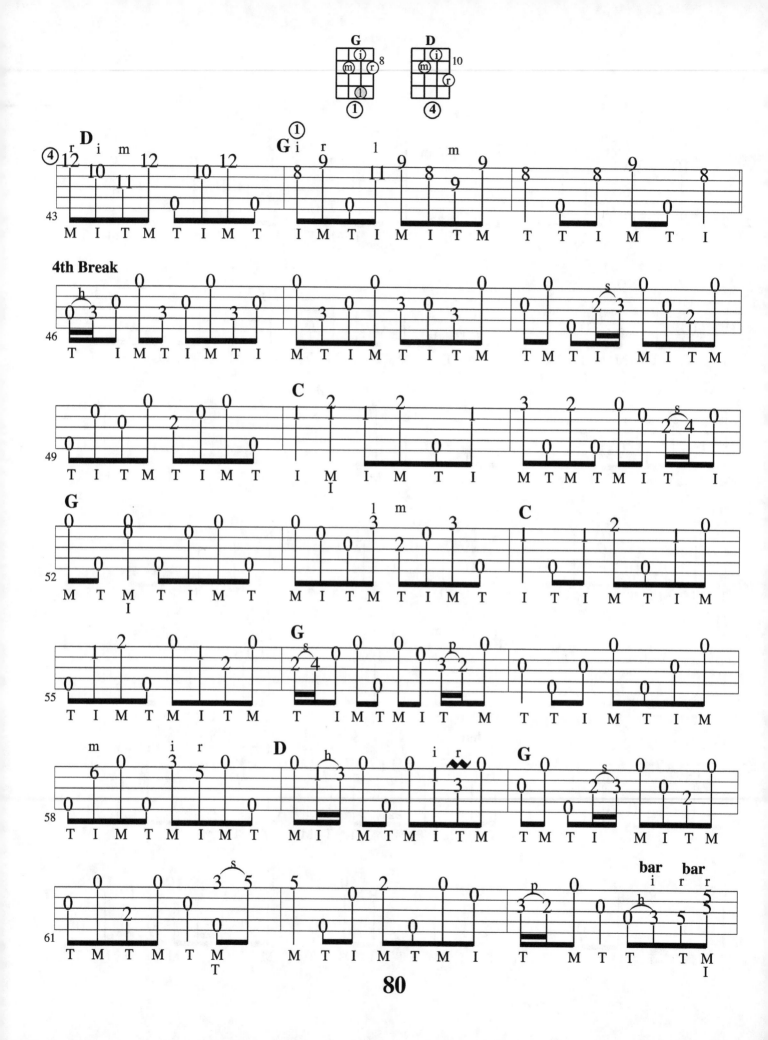

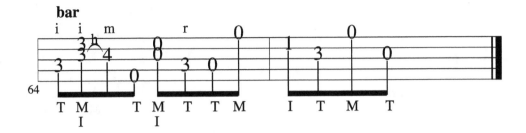

Roll On Buddy Notes

If you have worked through several songs in this book, you will see left hand patterns and chord shapes that are used in up the neck playing. The up the neck break to *Roll On Buddy* uses these patterns plus has a few variations.

Grandfather's Clock Notes

The fingering for the first break to *Grandfather's Clock* can be figured out from the left hand notation in the music. The second break will require more study and practice. In order to understand measures 46, 52, 54 and 63, which include forward and backward slides, study the examples for *Swing Low Sweet Chariot*.

Because we have not included chord diagrams, you will need to study the music more carefully. Stick with it and you will dramatically increase your knowledge of left hand fingering.

WILDWOOD FLOWER

Arr. by Geoff Hohwald

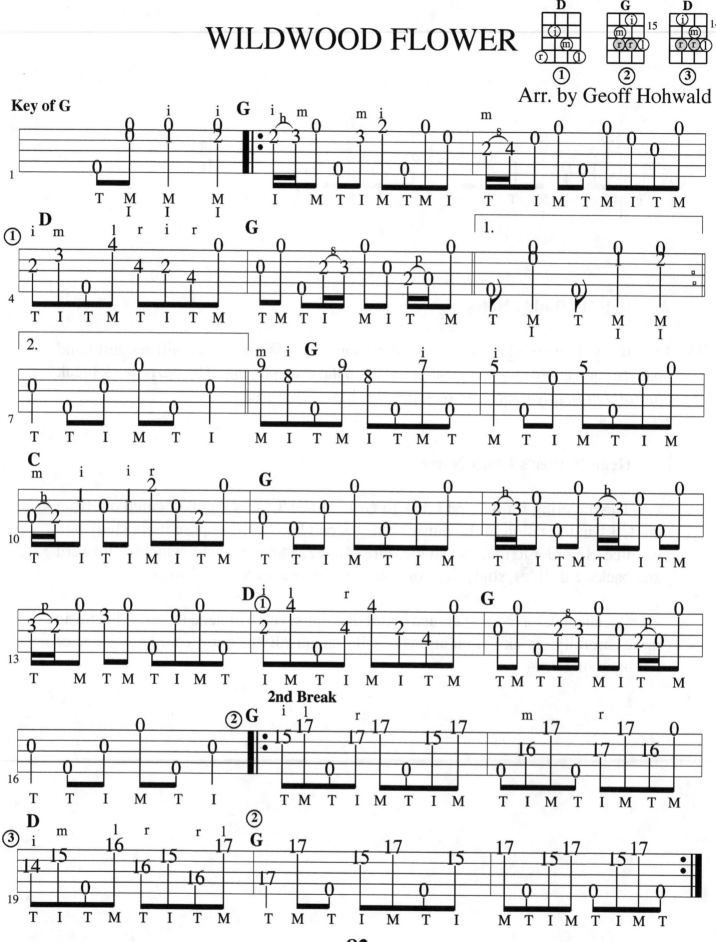

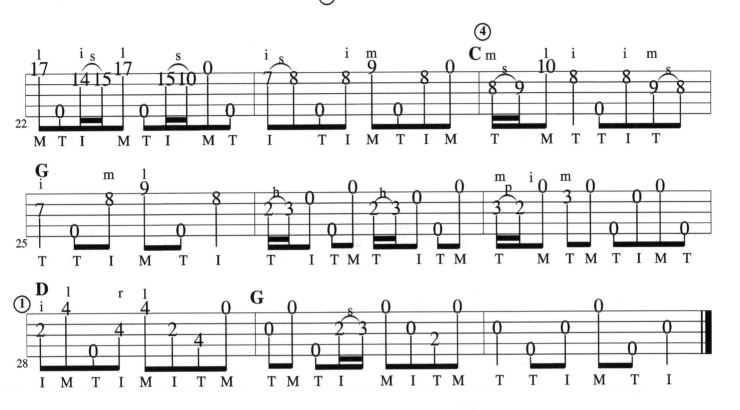

Wildwood Flower Notes

The main thing to notice in *Wildwood Flower* is that the second break is played using a high G position similar to that used in *Old Joe Clark*. This position is not widely used, but has been used in these two songs to provide a high break that contains the melody.

BILL CHEATUM

Arr. by Hohwald & McKinley

Key of G

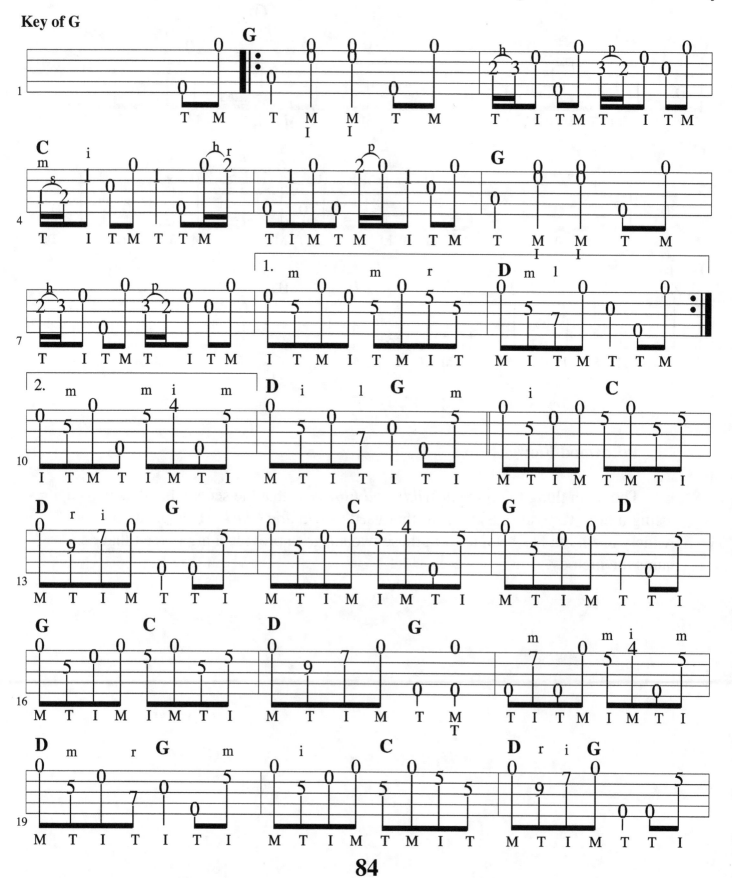

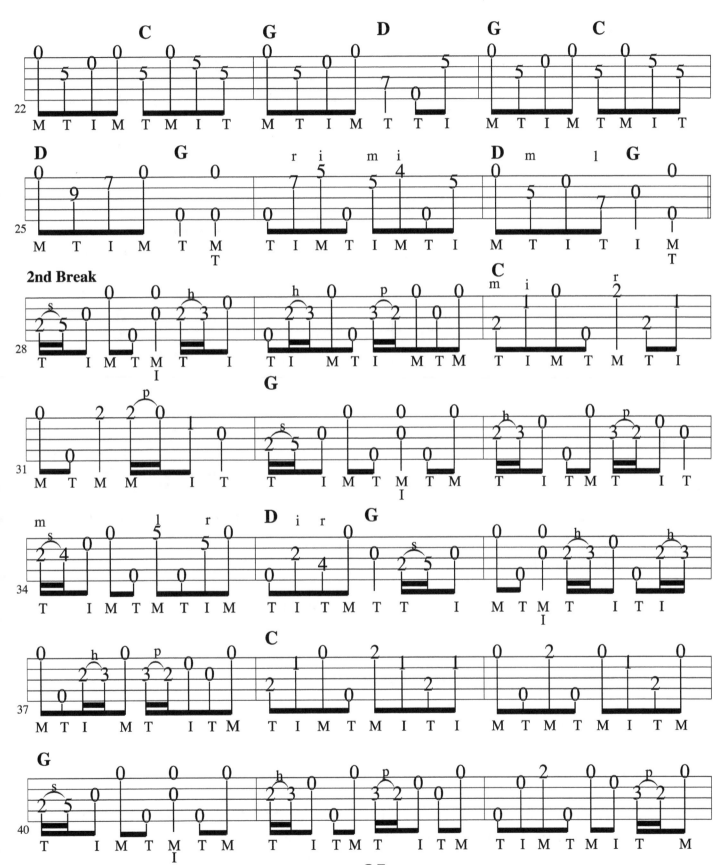

2nd Break

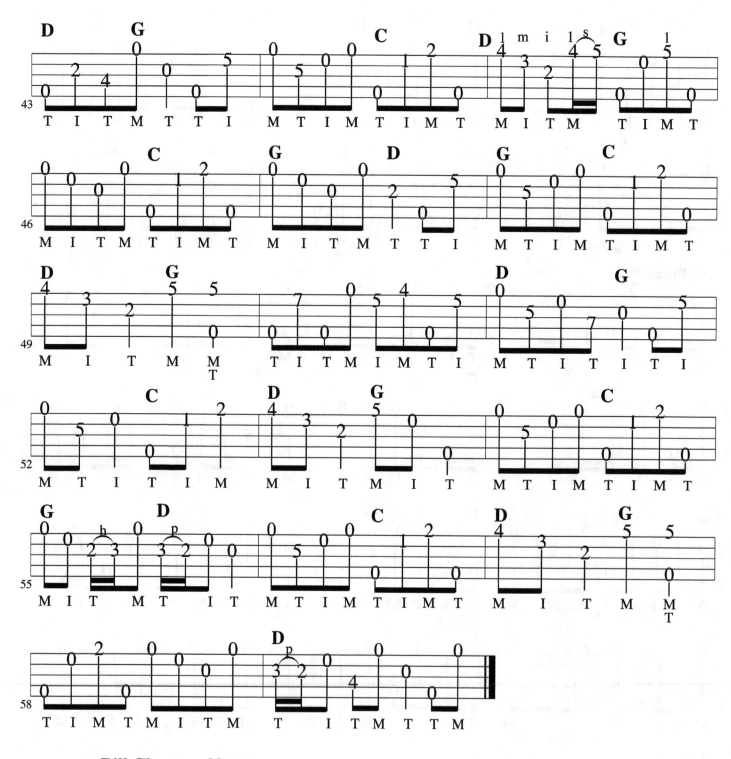

Bill Cheatum Notes

Bill Cheatum is primarily a melodic break. Notice the left hand fingering is usually much easier in melodic playing, but often involves more stretching.

86

KICKING MULE

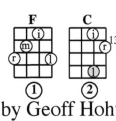

Arr. by Geoff Hohwald

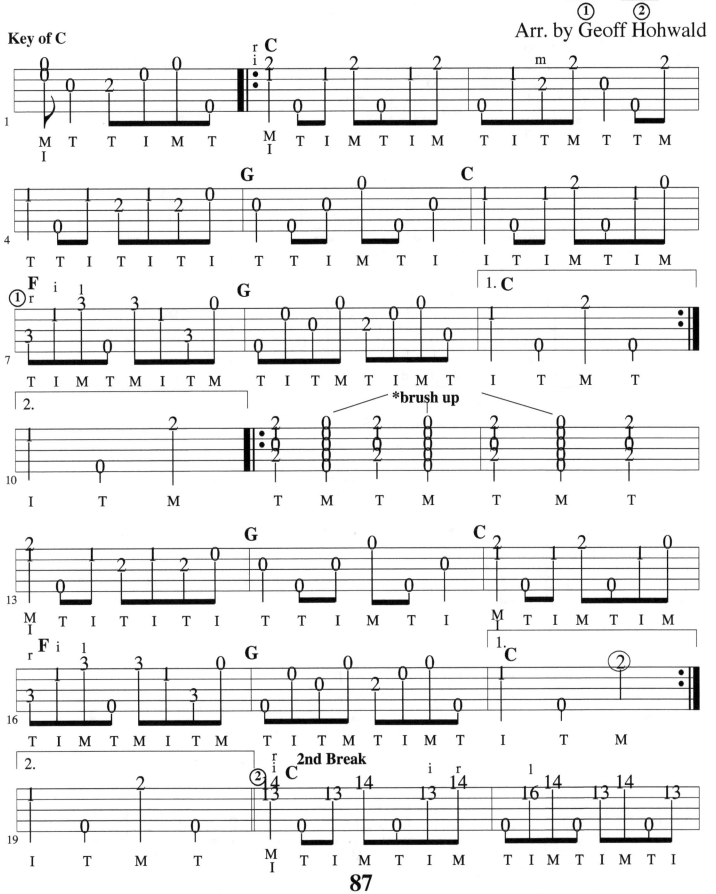

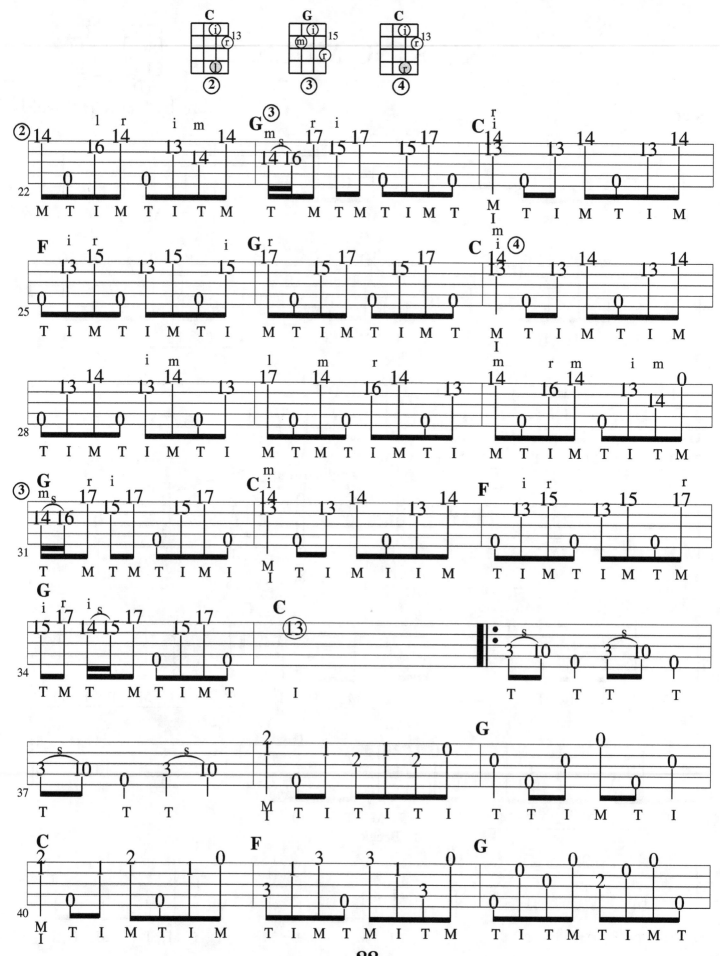

88

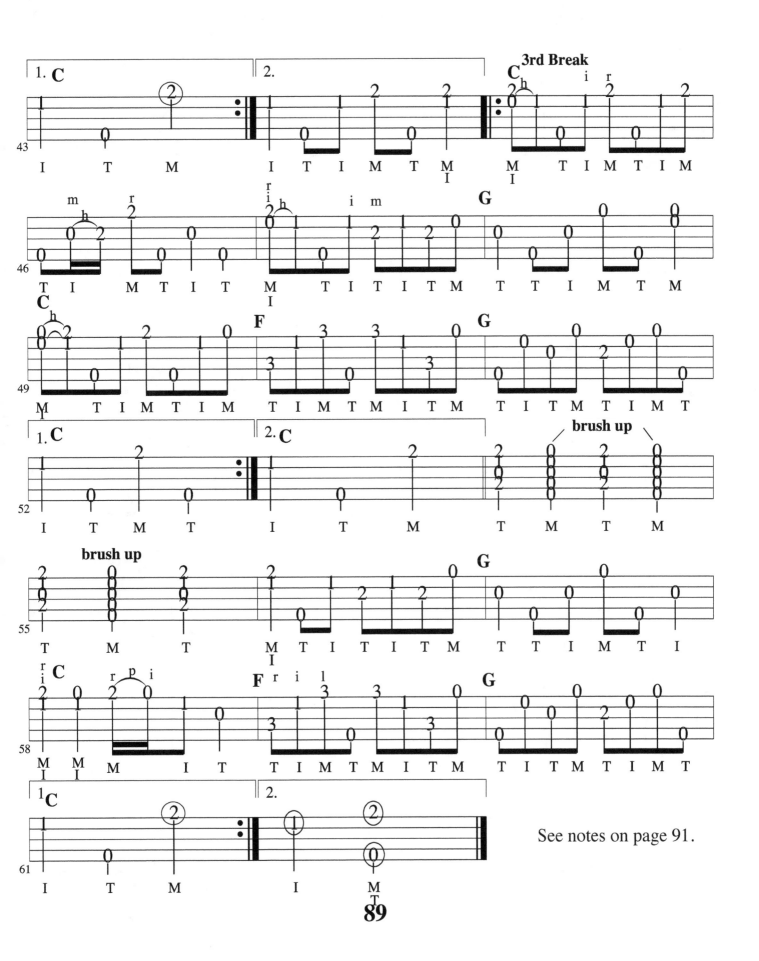

See notes on page 91.

89

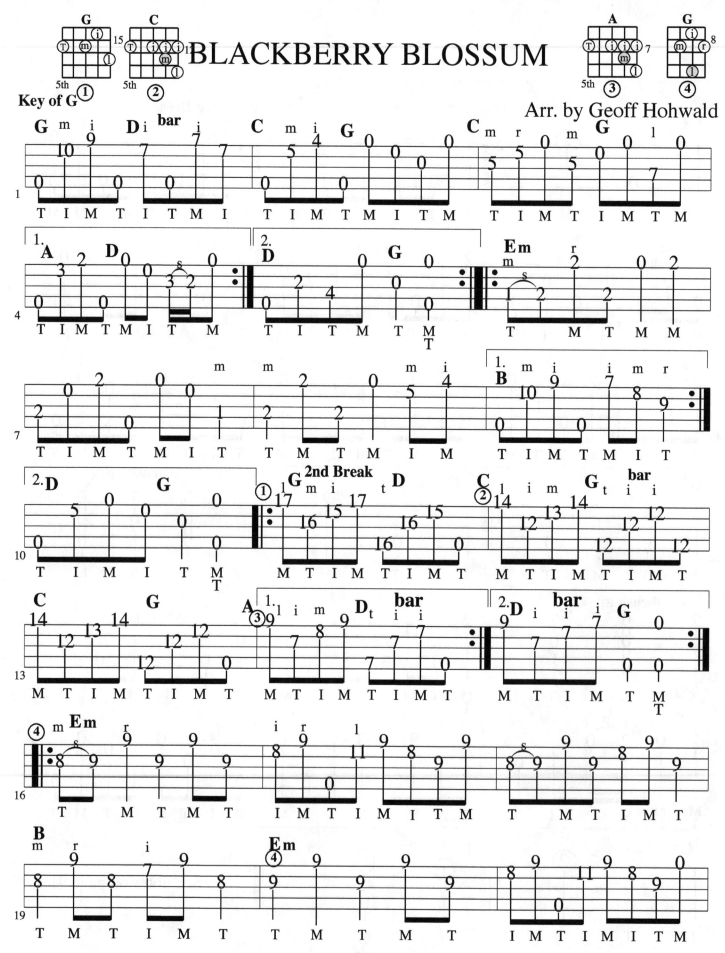

BLACKBERRY BLOSSUM

Arr. by Geoff Hohwald

Key of G

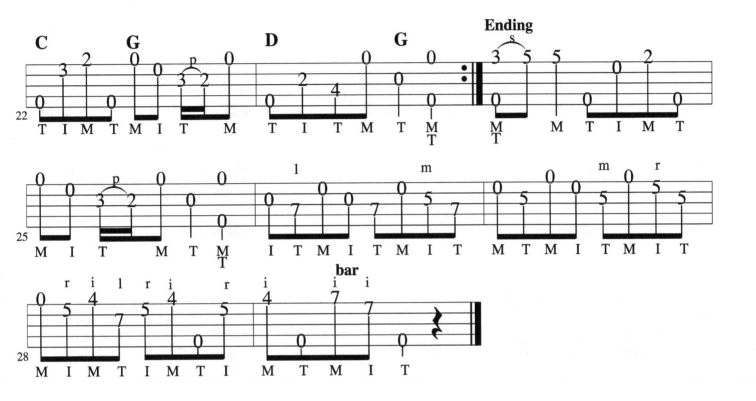

Blackberry Blossum Notes

The fingering for the first break of *Blackberry Blossom* is self explanatory. The fingerings for the second break are included in the tab. The second break is unique and sounds great. Pay particular attention to the different chord forms and try to change between them as smoothly as possible.

Kicking Mules Notes

Kicking Mule is played in the Key of C using C position chords. Notice in the up the neck playing, we are using the same shapes and forms for the left hand, but in different positions on the neck. To get the sound of the mule braying, we strum up on the strings between the bridge and the tail piece with the middle finger of the left hand. Compare the sound you get with the Audio Tracks.

Measures 23 and 31 - When sliding from the 3rd string 14th to the 16th fret, the entire shape moves, as opposed to just the notes on the 3rd string.

TRAIN 45

Arr. by Geoff Hohwald

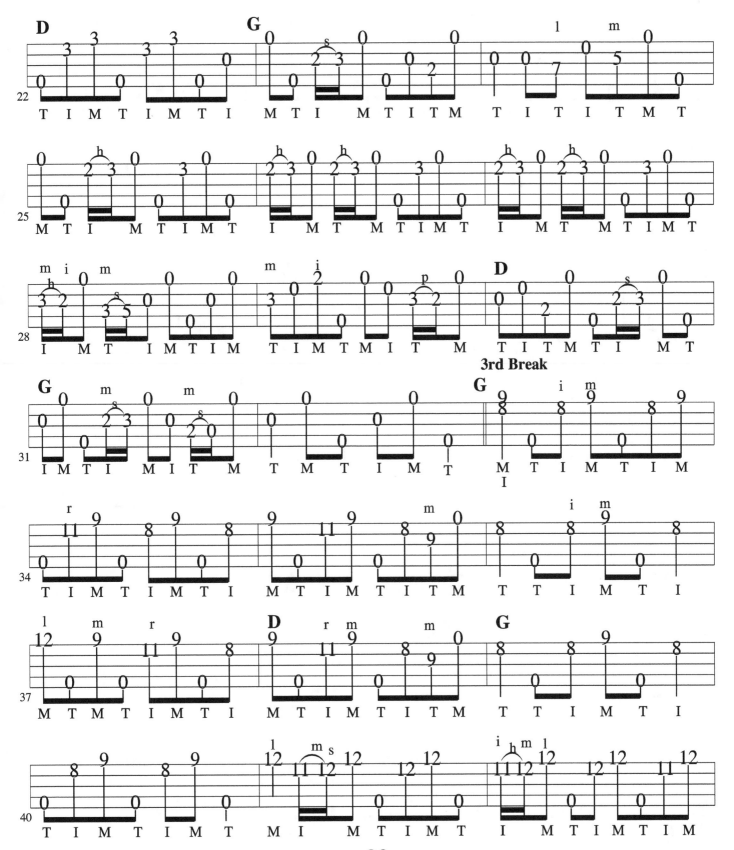

3rd Break

93

94

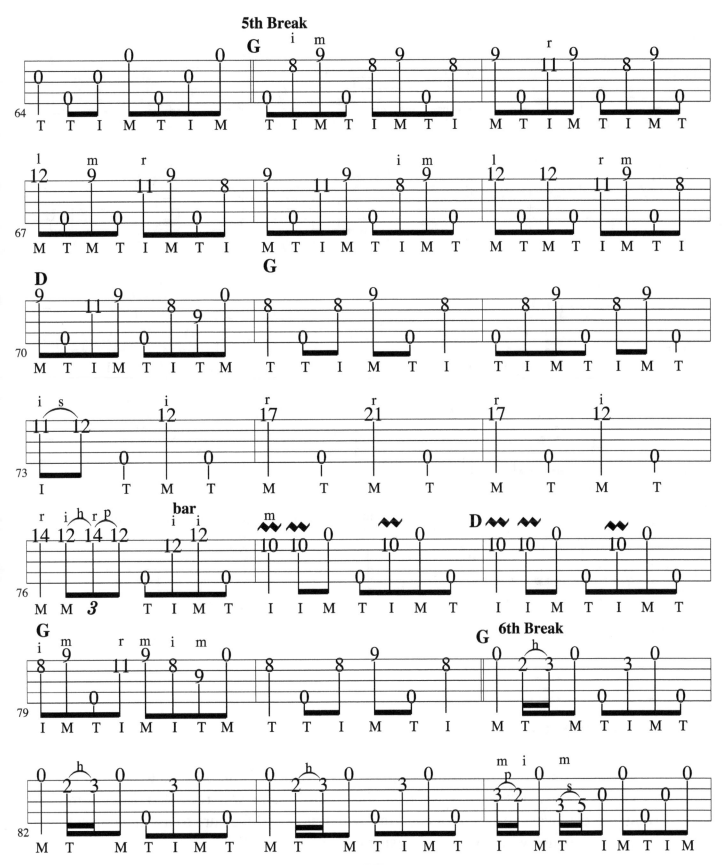

95

Train 45 Notes

This arrangement contains lots of percussive licks that can be used to add interest to other songs. The slow version on the Audio Tracks was recorded at 45 bpm so that you can hear the accent of each individual note. Make sure to use the correct left hand fingerings when playing measures 33-40 and 65-72.

SALT RIVER

Arr. by Hohwald & McKinley

Key of A
Capo 2nd Fret

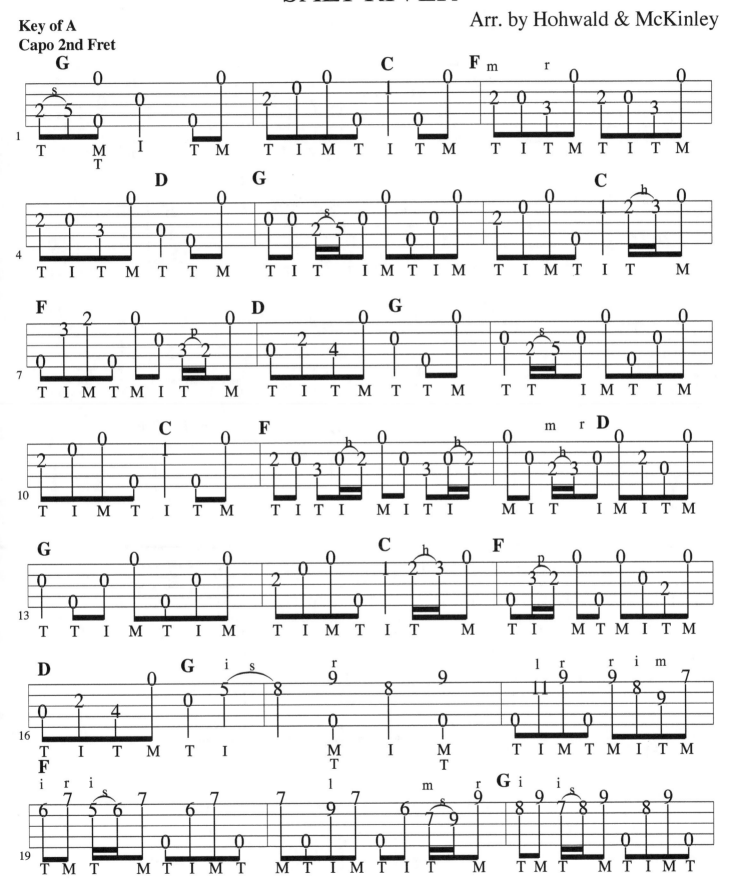

97

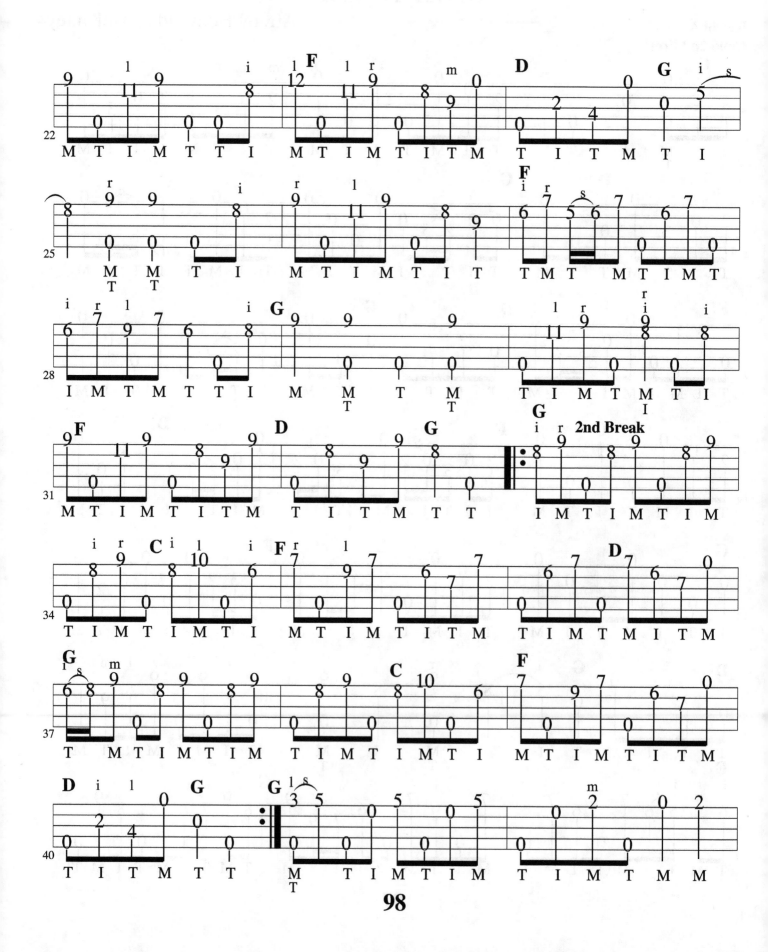

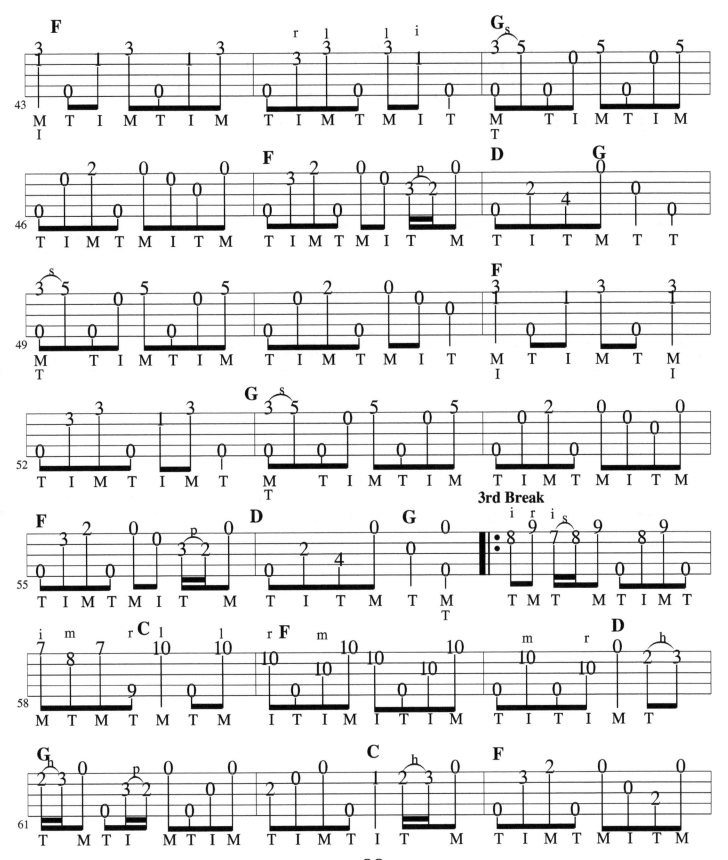

99

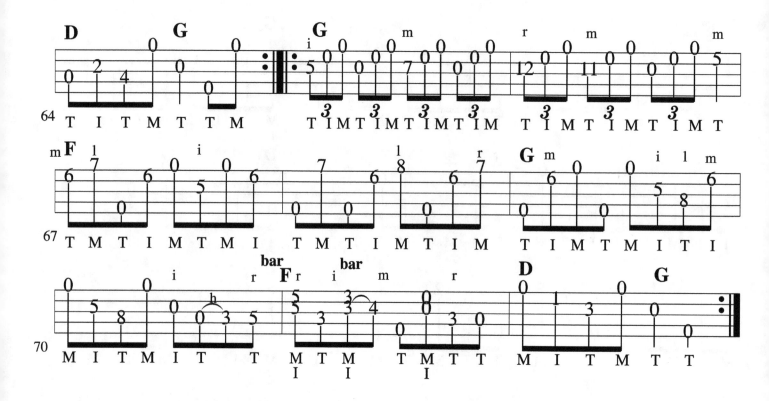

Salt River Notes

Salt River contains 3 breaks with the first two being fairly straight forward. The third break, mostly created by Bill McKinley, is one of my favorites. Listen to the Audio Tracks and good luck.

PURE PLEASURE

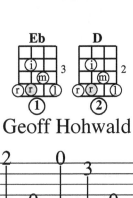

Geoff Hohwald

Key of G

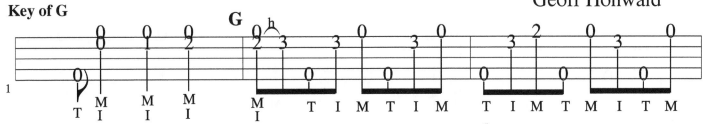

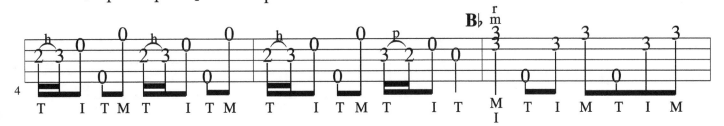

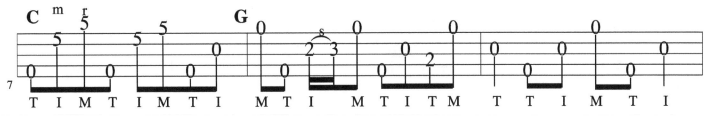

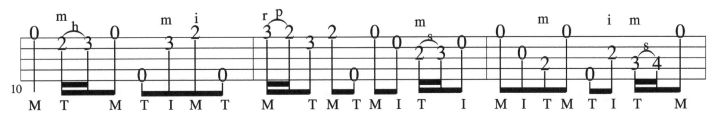

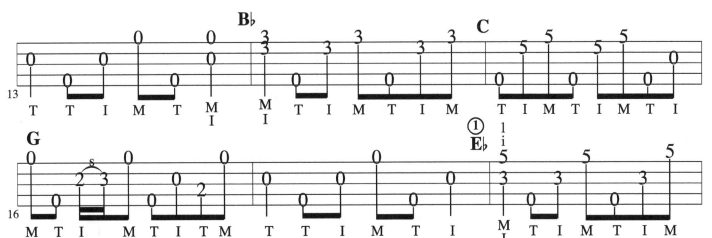

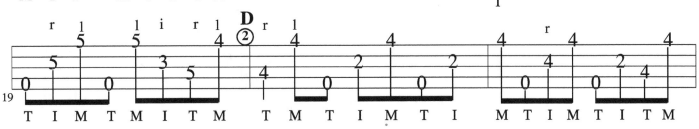

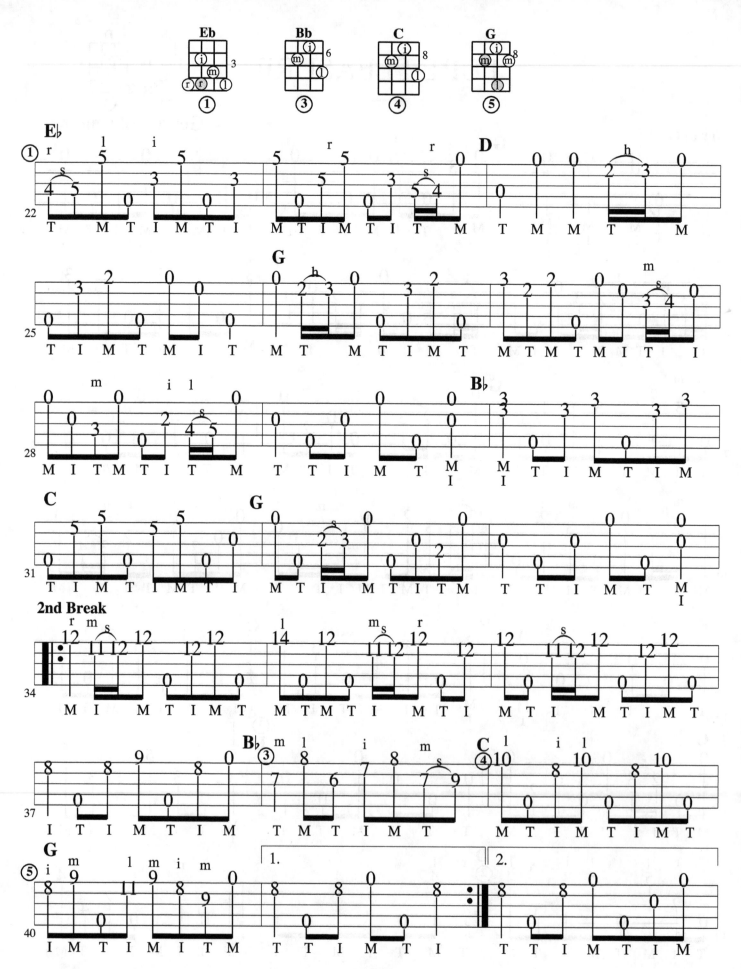

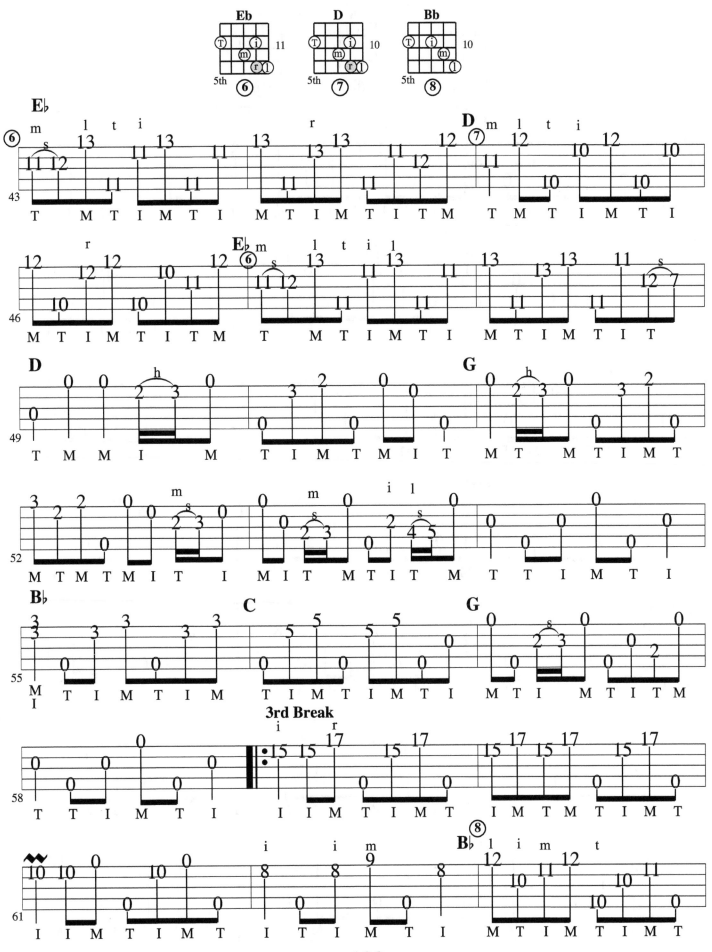

103

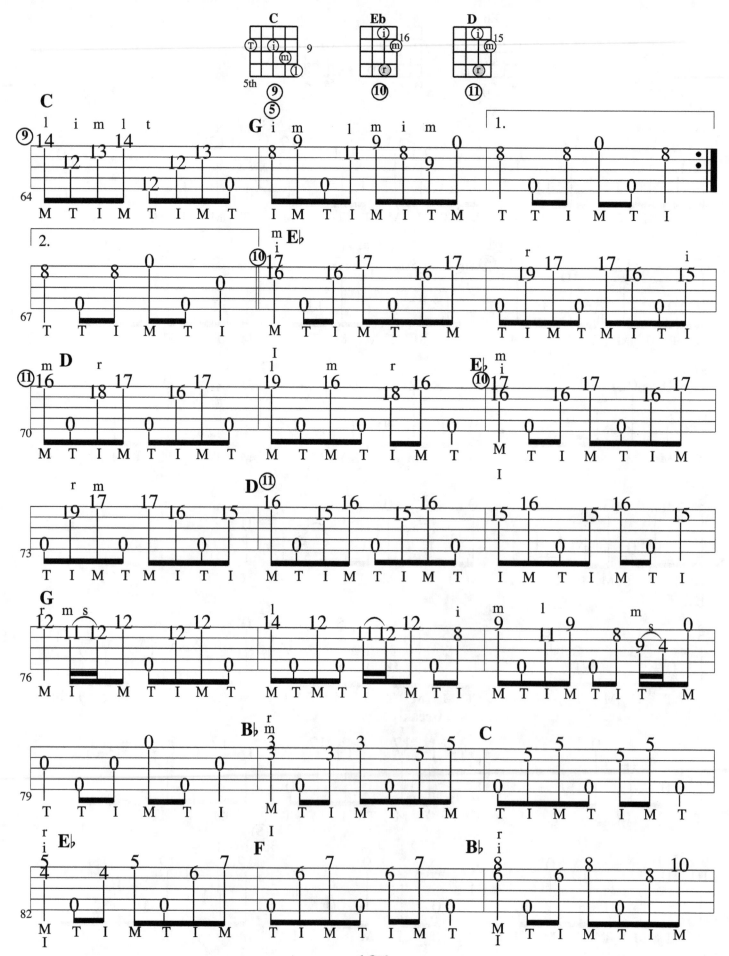

104

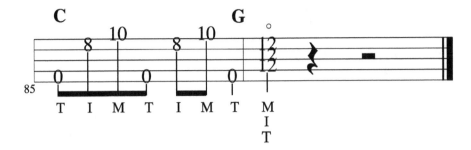

Pure Pleasure Notes

Pure Pleasure is included because I wanted to use a song I had written. Emory Gordy, Jr. was helping The Greater Atlanta Bluegrass Band, of which I was a member, record a tape. He asked each band member to write a song and this was my contribution. I couldn't think of a title and was discussing this with Emory at a horse race where we were performing. He suggested naming the song after the horse who won the next race, which happened to be *Pure Pleasure*.

APPENDIX

UP THE NECK FINGERINGS

We'll explore the most common left hand finger positions that are used up the neck of the banjo to make chords. Each chord form will be referred to as a shape.

G@7th Fret *

Primary Shape

G

This is used mostly for vamping.

Variation 1

G

This permits the little finger to note the 12th fret while leaving the index & middle fingers in place. The middle & little fingers float in this position.
Train 45 (36-37)

Variation 1A

G

This is used at the option of the player.
Train 45 (43)

Variation 2

G

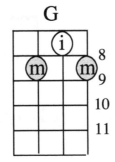

The middle & little fingers float.
Sitting On Top of the World (35)

Variation 3

G

The index finger is stationary and the middle finger floats.
Train 45 (38)

Variation 4

G

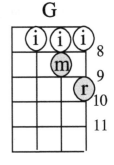

The index finger bars the first 3 strings and the middle & ring fingers float.
Dixie (17), *Little Maggie* (18)

* All of these positions can be used in C by moving to the 12th fret or D by moving to the 14th fret.

C@8th Fret

Primary Shape

C

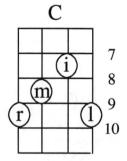

7
8
9
10

This is used primarily for playing rhythm.

Variation 1

C

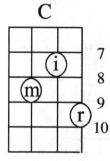

7
8
9
10

See notes below.

Variation 1A

C

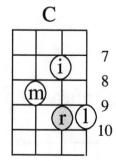

7
8
9
10

Variation 2

C

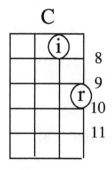

8
9
10
11

Boil Them Cabbage (18)

Many C licks start with a slide on the 3rd string with the whole shape on the fretboard even though only one note is being played. The whole shape then slide up one fret. *Pallet On Your Floor* (22).

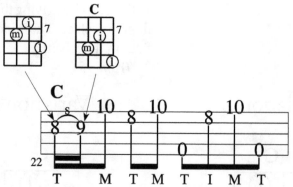

A similar left hand movement occurs 2 frets up in D in *Pretty Polly* (38).

D@2nd Fret

Primary Shape

D

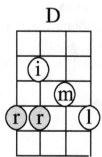

The ring finger floats. Examples - *John Hardy - Dark Hollow*

Flattening Fingers for Additional Notes

Study the following example - *Nine Pound Hammer* (31). This lick works over a D chord or a G chord.

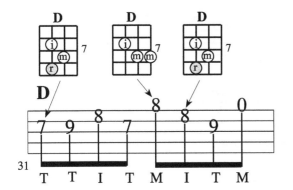

These chords shapes form a D or a G chord.

Flatten the middle finger on the 5th note to play the 1st string @ 8th fret.

In the following example, flatten the ring finger to play additional notes, *Pretty Polly* (70-71).

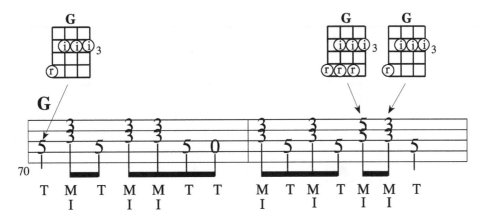

G Shape Choreography

Study and play through the following examples,

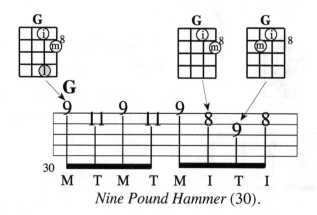

Nine Pound Hammer (30).

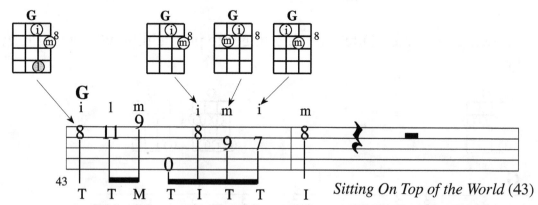

Sitting On Top of the World (43)

C Shape Choreography

Primary Shape

C

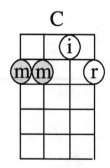

The middle finger floats.
Pallet On You Floor (3, 7)

Variation 1

C

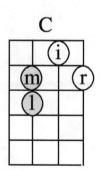

This is extremely hard, requiring a very strong
little finger, and is used for hammer on's and pull
offs. *Pallet On Your Floor* (35)

110

Two String Bars

In studying the tablature, look for these bar variations:

Variation 1

C

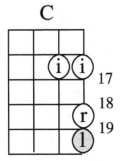

Ring and little finger float.
Little Maggie (42-43).

Variation 2

G

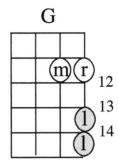

Little finger floats.
Pretty Polly (32).

Identifying Left Hand Patterns

Look for left hand patterns when playing up the neck.

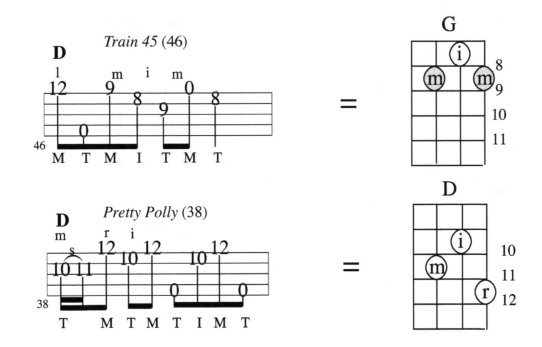

Identifying Left Hand Patterns

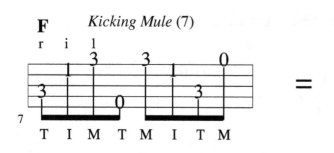
F *Kicking Mule* (7)

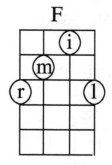
F

=

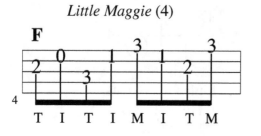
Little Maggie (4)
F

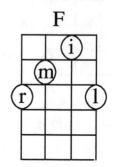
F

=

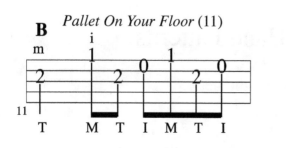
B *Pallet On Your Floor* (11)

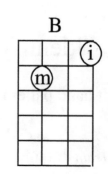
B

=

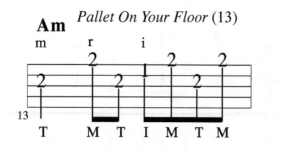
Am *Pallet On Your Floor* (13)

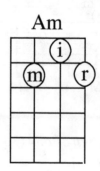
Am

=

Transition Notes

Look for the last note of a measure that's used for a transition into the next chord as follows:

Black Mountain Rag (68-69)

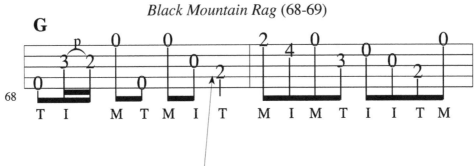

The last note of measure 68 is a quarter note, which gives you extra time for the left hand movement to the next position.

Pretty Polly (58-59)

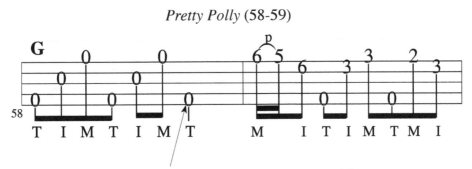

An open string gives you time to get to the next position.

Soldier's Joy (5)

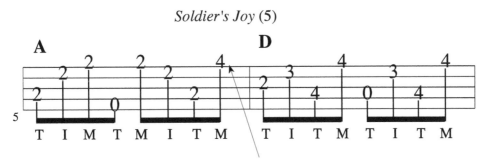

The last note of the first measure is part of the chord in the next measure.